CHRONOGRAM
CODE

Startling Discoveries Of Endtime Predictions For This Decade
Deciphered From The Encoded Scriptures Sealed For Centuries

Dr. Robert E. Mawire

Master Plan Books

Unless otherwise noted all scripture references in this book have been obtained from **The New King James**

First Edition printed November, 2011

Chronogram Code
ISBN 0-978-0-6155654-3-9

Master Plan Books
P.O. Box 895
Fort Worth, Texas 76101
Email: wrnoradio@mailup.net

Cover Design by Caleb D. Mawire

Printed by: The Williamson Printing Corporation
                6700 Denton Drive
                Dallas, TX 75235

ACKNOWLEDGMENT

First and foremost I give all praise and thanksgiving to the Lord Jesus Christ, the Master Planner and date setter of the ages. He sent His Angel Gabriel to reveal to Daniel the prophet the end of days. He was told to conceal and seal the message until the terminal generation.

The seal has been broken, the enigma has been revealed, the mystery unveiled, now before you in the pages of this book the code is decoded and doomsday revealed as God promised.

I am greatly indebted to the countless writers throughout the ages who labored to leave us a wealth of evidence to prove the infallibility of the Messianic Clock embedded in the Holy Scriptures.

I am grateful to the Good News family who encouraged me to press on and finish the work and to Larry Hopkins who encouraged me to rework the manuscript, which led to seemingly endless revisions.

It would be remiss if I failed to acknowledge John Peter, Joe Galindo, Marty Moore, Dean Spurlock, Edd and Junia Bettes, Yves Michiels, Reggie Kelly, Jim Borchert, Pat and Jack Godfrey, Denise Mpinga and many others too numerous to mention who prayed and encouraged me to get the job done.

Special appreciation should be expressed to Bill Noble, Jay Scheideman, Hyman White, Bruce Johnston and Wright Brewer for their invaluable help.

I am most grateful to Ray Bentley whose contribution and encouragement proved almost infinite. I express my deepest gratitude and admiration to him and to his wife, Vicki. Such friendships are made in heaven. I greatly value them as a gift from God.

Grateful acknowledgement is made to Gina and Andy Puterbaugh for their kairos assistance.

My profound thanks go to Steve and Anna Sappington and Shirley Langdon for helping in the editing process to make ready this work for publication.

All those who encouraged and assisted me come from a varied theological spectrum, from pre-trib, mid-trib and post-trib, since the content of this book is critical for every believer alive today. They felt that it is important to get this message out because the Lord is coming back soon.

I continued to draw special sustenance from the constant support during this protracted period of preparing this work from my siblings, Kenneth, Kingston, John, Betty, Norah, Julia, Rachel and Suzan for their undaunted support and encouragement and my immediate family, Jonathan and Devon, Caleb, Stephen and Annaly.

My most affectionate appreciation goes to my beloved wife Janet, whose hours of dedication spent over the computer keyboard typing and retyping the manuscript, patiently, prayerfully and skillfully has made this work possible.

Finally, I would like to thank you, the reader, for your participation in the adventure, for you are the one with an appointment with destiny. I present to you evidence attested by over three hundred scriptures that demand your verdict for "the time is at hand". You have been startled by world affairs, shocked by economic meltdowns, and perplexed by unprecedented natural disasters. The Word of God gives the only rock-hard truth about what is going on today.

This book presents a comprehensive digest of the timetable of future events detailed and their foretelling scriptures. Since the divine timelines are superimposed on top of each other like wheels within wheels. We present the big picture in the introduction first, then throughout the book we zoom in on each timeline for a closer look. As the predictions contained in the Chronogram Code constitute an immediate future here and now.

As the predictions contained in the Chronogram Code constitute an immediate danger facing the reader.

Please note that all Biblical references are listed at the back of the book in number order. Footnotes are at the bottom of the page. May God richly bless you as we travel together into our immediate future on this time machine, the Messianic Clock as encoded in the Chronogram Code. The Greek word Chronogram means the passage of time.

TABLE OF CONTENTS

INTRODUCTION...1
Prophetic Signposts
Prophetic Time Maps
Problems With Ancient Extra Biblical Chronology
The Gabriel Sealed Time Template Unsealed
Noahian Time Template
The Genesis Time Template
The Messianic Clock Cut Short
This Generation Has An Appointment With Destiny
Doomsday Can Be Postponed

CHAPTER ONE...19
THE PROPHETIC SIGN POSTS
The Current Signs Of The Time Confirm The Messianic Clock To Doomsday
The Future Has Been Prerecorded
This Is The Terminal Generation
It Is Critical To Know The Future
This Is The Hour For Preparation
NASA Warning Of The Approaching Interstellar Storm
The Day Of The Rapture Is Not Known
Signs Of The Rapture
Chart: The Terms The New Testament Uses To Describe The Rapture

CHAPTER TWO..33

> MESSIANIC CLOCK: THE PROPHETIC TIME MAPS
>
> *Modern Time Map Events*
> *Drought Conditions For Foreign Occupiers Of The Holy Land Predicted*
> *The Destruction Of Iraq (Ancient Babylon) By "Operation Desert Storm"*
> *And "The Coalition of the Willing" Was Predicted 2,500 Years Ago*
> *Description Of A Modern Air Force 2,500 Years Ago*
> *Partitioning Of The Holy Land By The General Assembly Of The United*
> *Nations In 1947*
> *The Body Of Hitler Will Not Be Found*
> *Age Of Global And Space Travel*
> *Age Of Knowledge Explosion*
> *Unprecedented Moral Erosion As A Sign Of The End Of Days*

CHAPTER THREE..43

> THE MESSIANIC CLOCK: LOST AND REPLACED BY THE
> HISTORICAL CALENDAR DISTORTIONS
>
> *The Origin Of The Jewish Calendar Is Not Biblical*
> *The Historical Parallelism Between The Babylonian And Hebrew Calendars*
> *The Handwriting On The Wall*

CHAPTER FOUR..55

> THE MESSIANIC CLOCK: ANCIENT JEWISH WEDDING PARADIGM
>
> *The Feasts of the Lord*
> *The Feasts of the Lord as Historical Divine Appointments*
> *Historical Set Time for Judgment*

CHAPTER FIVE..59

    MESSIANIC CLOCK: THE GENESIS TIME TEMPLATE

    Creation Matrix

    Creation To Doomsday

    The Church Fathers Knew The Prophetic Time Map To Doomsday

    6,000 Years Preset Time From Creation To Doomsday

    Historical Dates For The Creation

    The Messianic Clock: Doomsday Preset From Creation

    Chart: The Messianic Clock: Genesis 7-Day Time Template To Doomsday

CHAPTER SIX..75

    ONE HUNDRED AND TWENTY JUBILEE YEARS TIME TEMPLATE

     TO DOOMSDAY

    Noah's Flood Historical Fact

    Chart: The Noahian Messianic Clock: 120 Jubilees From Creation To

    Doomsday

CHAPTER SEVEN...91

    THE DANIEL MESSIANIC CLOCK: BREAKING THE SEAL OF THE

     ENIGMA OF THE AGES

CHAPTER EIGHT...95

    THE MESSIANIC CLOCK: THE DANIEL ENIGMA UNVEILED

    THE FOUR EMPIRES PREDICTED TO RULE BEFORE THE

    ADVENT OF THE MILLENNIAL KINGDOM

    Chart: Daniel's Description Of The World Empires

CHAPTER NINE...105

    THE GABRIEL MESSIANIC CLOCK: THE SIGNS OF THE TIMES ARE

    ALIGNING FOR THE FIRST TIME IN HISTORY

    This Generation Will Understand Daniel's Sealed Message

CHAPTER TEN..**111**

> THE GABRIEL MESSIANIC CLOCK: FROM CYRUS' DECREE TO
> JESUS' CRUCIFIXION– 483 YEARS UNVEILED
>
> *The First Decree To Restore Jerusalem And The First Advent Of Christ*
> *The Gabriel Messianic Clock: From The Destruction Of The Solomonic*
> *Temple To The Building Of The Dome Of The Rock, The Abomination Of*
> *Desolation - 1,290 Years*
> *Chart: Destruction Of The Solomonic Temple To The Building Of The Dome*
> *Of The Rock / Abomination Of Desolation - 1,290 Years*

CHAPTER ELEVEN..**117**

> THE MESSIANIC CLOCK: FROM THE DOME OF THE ROCK
> TO DOOMSDAY – 1,335 YEARS UNVEILED
>
> *Chart: The Daniel Messianic Clock: Destruction Of The First Temple To*
> *Doomsday*

CHAPTER TWELVE..**121**

> THE MESSIANIC CLOCK: FROM THE SECOND DECREE BY
> SULEIMAN THE MAGNIFICENT TO RESTORE JERUSALEM
> TO DOOMSDAY – 490 YEARS UNVEILED
>
> *Parallelism Between Christ's And Antichrist Timeline*
> *Chart: The Messianic Clock: Second Decree To Restore Jerusalem*
> *To The New Jerusalem - 490 Years Decreed*

CHAPTER THIRTEEN..**133**

> GABRIEL MESSIANIC CLOCK: FROM THE CONFIRMATION OF
> THE ISRAELI PEACE TREATY TO DOOMSDAY – 7 YEARS

CHAPTER FOURTEEN..**137**

> THE MESSIANIC CLOCK: FIRST ADVENT TO SECOND ADVENT
> –2,000 YEARS UNVEILED
>
> *Chart: Messianic Clock: Two Thousand Year Grace Dispensation*
> *From The Baptism Of Jesus Christ To Consummation*

CHAPTER FIFTEEN...149

    COUNTDOWN TO ARMAGEDDON UNVEILED

    Chart: The Messianic Clock: The Prophetic Events 2012 A.D.- 2026 A.D.

    Chart: Gabriel Messianic Clock: Second Destruction Of Jerusalem To
    Second Coming Of Christ

CHAPTER SIXTEEN...155

    THE GABRIEL MESSIANIC CLOCK: UNVEILS THE CELESTRIAL SIGNS TO
    MARK THE BEGINNING OF SORROWS AND THE END OF TIME (2012 –
    2026 A.D.)

    Astronomical Alignment on Rosh Hashanah

    Chart: Signs In The Heavens During The Sixty Ninth And Seventieth
    Week Of Daniel

CHAPTER SEVENTEEN...161

    THE MESSIANIC CLOCK: THE GLORY OF GOD RETURNS INTO THE THIRD
    TEMPLE ON TEMPLE MOUNT

    Chart: The Messianic Clock: Jerusalem Epicenter/Temple Mount
    Ground Zero – Four Thousand Year History

CHAPTER EIGHTEEN...169

    THE DANIEL MESSIANIC CLOCK: ALIGNMENT WITH THE MOSES' TORAH
    VERSES/ YEAR CODE PROPHECY

    Mystery Babylon: The Revived Roman Empire
    Numerical Value Of The Jewish Year 5788
    Chart: Messianic Clock: Torah Verses/Year Correlation
    Chart: Messianic Clock: Torah Verses/Year Correlation 2020-2027 A.D.

CHAPTER NINETEEN...181

    MESSIANIC CODE: IN THE YEAR 2026 A.D. JULIAN CALENDAR ENCODED
    THE CONSUMMATION OF HISTORY

CHAPTER TWENTY...183
THE MESSIANIC CLOCK: THE PRESERVATION OF THE SAINTS
FROM THE GREAT TRIBULATION
Kept Away Before Being Taken Away

CHAPTER TWENTY-ONE...199
THE MANIFESTATION OF THE SONS OF GOD
The Greatest Harvest Of All Time

CHAPTER TWENTY-TWO...211
THE MESSIANIC CLOCK: THE RAPTURE
Imminent Return Of Christ
The Wrath Of God
Second Coming Of Christ
 Chart: Messianic Predictions: Two Comings Of The Messiah, Prophecies
Concerning Christ's Coming

CHAPTER TWENTY-THREE...219
THE MILLENNIUM KINGDOM
The New Heaven And New Earth
The New Jerusalem Replaces The Old Jerusalem
 Chart: When Shall The End Of These Wonders Be?

CONCLUSION..227

THE WAY OF SALVATION...231

SCRIPTURE INDEX..233

BIBLIOGRAPHY..243

INTRODUCTION

This book addresses the most crucial question being asked for the first time by people in the midst of present global financial meltdown and political upheaval: "Are these the last days?" A decade ago, this subject was reserved for religious fanatics. But now scientists and intellectuals alike, on Main Street and on Wall Street, are predicting the demise of western civilization, and the death of the American dollar.

A close look at the ancient predictions in the Bible will provide answers to our present quandary. This book assembles the pieces and uncovers the staggering predictions for our times.

The aim of this book is to give its readers a Biblical understanding of the signs of the times and the infallible calendar for the end of days. The period is exact and precise, encrypted in Daniel's secret code. The doomsday deciphered from the Daniel cryptogram is fast approaching. Down through the corridor of time, Biblical prophecy and dateline have never failed. History validates Hebrew (Biblical) predictions.

We will discover that the timeline of history is not defined by the rise and fall of great civilizations, but rather by the predetermined purposes of God, revealed in His Holy Word. Everything was planned before the foundation of the world, and initiated at the dawn of time. History is the unfolding of the divine blueprint of the ages, preset and prerecorded.

Readers seeking to find answers in the midst of gut wrenching perplexity and the depression induced by fear of unknown perils can turn to the infallible Word of God. Someone was sent from eternity to tell the prophets the ominous future that stands before us in these last days.

PROPHETIC SIGNPOSTS

God has posted signposts in every age to help the people of God discern what time it is. The prophetic timeline has markers from the dawn of time to doomsday. The future and the doomsday date have been foretold. The dateline of the ages, encoded in Daniel, is finally decoded, pinpointing the precise doomsday concealed in the Holy Scriptures.

With amazingly perfect precision, the current signs of the times synchronize with the prophetic timetable. Everything going on in the world is on schedule. The present world affairs clearly demonstrate the fulfillment, precisely at the appointed time, the events that were predicted. It is important to realize that we are living in a crucial time in history, as foretold in the sacred Word of God. This generation has an appointment with destiny. The signs of the time are everywhere. There is no need to be disenchanted: the King is coming with the eternal Kingdom. These are the signs of the imminent Advent of the Millennium Kingdom.

This generation must look beyond the present gloom and doom to the coming glorious new age. Readers of this book will understand why it is not a time to be fearful, but a time to have joyous anticipation of a brighter new day, destined to arrive in our generation as predicted by the prophets of old.

PROPHETIC TIME MAPS

For Christians today, perhaps our most important discovery is that the Bible gives us the countdown from creation to doomsday, clearly to help us to prepare for the transition to glory. You will know how much time is left before the end of time. God is a date setter. In the past 6000 years of recorded human history, Biblical prophecies have been fulfilled at the precise predicted datelines.

Biblical prophecy harmonizes in every case with extra-Biblical records that have been discovered, with no exception. The same is the case today: we are on an infallible divine schedule to doomsday.

The Bible provides modern readers clear, solid, exact previews of the headlines of tomorrow: a literal sequential view with an infallible dateline. In His Word, God revealed His grand plan from creation to doomsday, because He is a date setter. He tells us the origin of the universe, the creation of man, the fall, the redemption and the dateline to the new heaven and new earth. Thus beyond the pain of the present world, God gives mankind hope in a world full of suffering. Everything is going as planned and on time. We will soon be home in glory.

The prophetic time maps encoded in the Word of God are both explicit and implicit. God is not the author of confusion. Each prophetic time map correlates and culminates at the exact preset termination date. Throughout history, the Messianic Clock has portrayed precision timing for every predicted event. The verifiable and accurate chronicles of history and the divine chronology are in perfect harmony.

PROBLEMS WITH ANCIENT EXTRA-BIBLICAL CHRONOLOGY

The past confusion in deciphering the Biblical timeline to doomsday has been because of the existence of numerous calendars and chronologies that are all different. In ancient times, various civilizations counted years from differing reference points. The Babylonians numbered years from the birth of King Sargon I, about 2637 B.C. The Greeks calculated according to the era of Olympiads, beginning in 776 B.C. The Romans used the date of the founding of Rome to number their years. A monk named Dionysius Exiguus, using a Roman calendar to calculate when Jesus was born, made our present Western calendar. The Jews adopted a false Babylonian calendar that counted from 3761 B.C,. as the beginning of time.

Gabriel gave the true Biblical timeline from creation to doomsday to Daniel, and he was told to seal it until the end of days, when the wise will understand it. It is the subject of this book. It is the centerpiece of Biblical chronology. The sealed message of Daniel has mystified generations until the appointed time of the end, as Gabriel said. God promised it would be revealed in the last days. The curtains have been lifted, the code has been broken, and the timeline from creation to doomsday has been revealed. Jesus said, "There is nothing secret that shall not be revealed." [1]

The Daniel time matrix and the Gabriel Messianic Clock are the keystones to understanding the Genesis and Noahian time templates. The Messianic Clock explains all the timelines and holds the key to our immediate future.

THE GABRIEL SEALED TIME TEMPLATE UNSEALED

Gabriel was sent by God to give Daniel the Messianic clock—the timeline to the end of days. He was told, "Go your way, Daniel, for these words are concealed and sealed up until the end time." [2] The message has been revealed because the consummation of all things is fast approaching. The ultimate future is here, as foretold to Daniel. We will share the decoded message, as it is critical for this hour. Neglecting or despising this concealed message would prove regrettably perilous.

In contrast to the popular opinion that no one knows when the world will end, the Bible reveals the date the world was created, and when it will end. God has a timetable to everything under heaven including doomsday. Daniel was given the period of the times of the Gentiles until doomsday and instructed to seal it and conceal it until God reveals it in the last days, "and the wise shall understand." [3] In the book of Amos it says, "Surely the Lord does nothing unless He reveals His secret counsel to His servants the prophets." [4]

The Apostle Paul says concerning doomsday, "You, brethren, are not in darkness that the day should overtake you like a thief." [5] The termination of time will not come as a thief in the night for the saints, because it is revealed in scripture. God said it. That settles the argument whether or not we believe it. "God cannot lie." He wants the saints to know when the end is coming.

THE NOAHIAN TIME TEMPLATE

More than four thousand years ago God said, "My spirit shall not strive with man forever because he also is flesh; nevertheless his days shall be one hundred and twenty years." [6] Did God lie, because it is now thousands of years since He said it, yet He is still striving with man! Or was this an enigma, a sealed and concealed timeline from creation to doomsday, when He will cease to strive with man? We will discover when the 120 years began and when they will end in our generation.

THE GENESIS TIME TEMPLATE

The six days of creation are God's concealed timetable from creation to doomsday. It is a divine blueprint of the ages. God tells the end from the beginning. Each creation day represents 1000 years in heaven's calculation of a day, as revealed in the book of second Peter chapter three verse eight. We will discuss in depth this grand design of the ages and the date when time began. Against this background we will see the big picture in the creation blueprint for the ages.

We will synchronize all Biblical timelines based upon clear scriptures, into what we call the "Messianic Clock." The Messianic Clock is a tabulation of all chronological data consistent with all extra-Biblical evidence of past prophetic fulfillments at the preset datelines in the scriptures.

I find no divergence between historical texts and Biblical texts. The enumeration of years from creation to doomsday is based upon the cumulative total of 6000 years from beginning to the end. God allocated six days of man's labor before the millennium rest is to occur in the seventh millennium.

There is a consistent, perfect precision of all Biblical timelines with the timeline given to Daniel by Gabriel. As we go through a total evaluation of historical and extra-Biblical evidence, it will become apparent in the Messianic Clock that there are no discrepancies or contradictions throughout the ages. Every prediction happened at the time foretold by the prophets. The Messianic Clock in this book has been attested to by 6000 years of precise timing.

It should be noted that such term as "timeline," "dateline," "timetable," "prophetic time map," and "time template" have been used interchangeably to constitute what is known in this book as the Messianic Clock. They are one and the same: the prophetic time matrix embedded in the Holy Scripture.

MESSIANIC CLOCK CUT SHORT

Jesus said the concealed timeline to doomsday given to Daniel "will be cut short for the sake of the elect." [7] This constitutes one of the reasons

He said that no one knows the exact day or hour when the Father will send His Son to take away the elect from the earth. He will suddenly come for the saints. He will rapture the elect to meet him in the air for the wedding feast of the Lamb. This event will last a shabuwa, or seven years, before His second coming, when He comes with the saints to set up the millennium Kingdom on the earth.

There is no allusion in Paul's elucidation that the saints will be fully aware when the coming of that day will be. He made it clear that it won't come as a thief in the night for the elect, since it is disclosed in scripture. The elect will know the timeframe, not the day and hour, as time will be shortened for the sake of the elect. Gabriel gave the date to Daniel that will be cut short. It is a privilege to be told what lies ahead of us before it takes place in reality.

Every event in the divine dateline that was predicted in the past has been on track, giving us the reason to believe that the prophetic timeline for the future is precise, as in times past. One should note that there is nothing ordinary about the Hebraic Bible. It has an intricate mathematical design, which makes it obvious that God is a God of order and precise timelines. He has preset and encoded in advance the world's historic calendar in His Word, for His children to decipher by divine illumination.

The Biblical text contains both (Peshat) literal and (Sod) future events encoded in a prophetic layer hidden in the narrative. For example, in the story of Haman's ten sons that were hanged, encoded in their names are the Hebrew letters tav, shin, and zayin. Hebrew letters each have a numerical value. When these three letters are added up, their total value is 5706. The Jewish year 5706 is the year 1946 in our Julian calendar. On October 16, 1946, ten Nazis were hanged on Hosanna Rabbah, "the Day of Final Verdict."

As we pierce the veil, we will discover that Biblical numbers are exact and literal. The devout Jews throughout the centuries held to the belief that in the Jewish year, 5708, God would gather the Jews back into their ancient homeland. They equated the torah verse with the Jewish year. They deciphered the encoded message in Torah verse, 5708, which says, "Then the Lord your God will restore you from captivity and have compassion on you, and will gather you again from the peoples where the Lord your God has scattered you." [8] The Jewish year, 5708, in the Julian calendar is 1948. The Jews were restored as a nation back into their land after nearly two thousand years in the Diaspora, as foretold in this passage.

The year of Israel's dispersion, 70 A.D., was encoded in Jesus' words in Matthew 24 when He said, "Jerusalem shall be destroyed." The Hebrew numerical value of His words foretold it would be in the year 70 A.D. There was not one believer left in Jerusalem when Titus destroyed it, since they knew it in advance, according to Josephus.

The Apostle John had a student named Polycarp who discovered the word *lateinos* in the numerical value of 666, the number of the Antichrist. It means the revival of the Roman Empire as the final Empire prior to Christ's return. In 1957 the Treaty of Rome revived the Roman Empire. This clearly predicts the Japhetic domination of the New World Order in the last days. Biblical texts contain startling revelations, infallible predictions, consistent continuity and unassailable unity.

The pages of the Bible contain classified information concerning the end of days. It is an indisputable fact that the Bible reveals the consummation of all things, since Jesus said, "I told you all things." [9]

This book endeavors to decode the critical signs of the time and the climactic and ominous events that will soon dominate our immediate future. The challenge of the hour for every living person is to find answers to these questions: What time is it, how much time do we still have before doomsday, and what does this decade hold for us? This is the decade of destiny. Scripture interpreting scripture will answer all these questions. The Word of God gives us real answers. These are the final days on earth.

THIS GENERATION HAS AN APPOINTMENT WITH DESTINY

The Messianic Clock reveals that we are standing at the brink of eternity. The countdown to doomsday has begun. The fate of this planet is at stake; an epic contest is drawing ever nearer. These are the last days. We are already experiencing the shock waves of the coming age, the footsteps of the coming Messiah.

We are daily confronted with bizarre political intrigues. We are fast descending into chaos; momentous events are catching our attention daily-paradigm shifts in the global political landscape. All the signs of the times are pointing to the end of the world. The pages of this book are a clarion call to action.

These are the days of tumult. People are looking for a Messiah. Self-made Messiahs are rising, presuming to hold the answers to our global problems. The pretensions of these persons are deceiving many. During the first Advent of Jesus, there was a mood of expectancy for the sudden appearance of the Messiah, and as a result, many imposters rose.

Dr. Luke mentions one of those imposters called Simon, who had a huge following:

> "But there was a certain man called Simon, who previously practiced sorcery in the city and astonished the people of Samaria, claiming that he was someone great, to whom they all gave heed, from the least to the greatest, saying, "This man is the great power of God."[10]

Secular historians have recorded the activities and teaching of many of these false Messiahs. Josephus wrote, "The land was overrun with magicians, seducers and impostors, who drew the people after them in multitudes into solitudes and deserts to see signs and miracles which they promised to show the power of God. A certain impostor named Theudas persuaded a great number to follow him to the river Jordan, which he claimed would divide for them passage." Many of these impostors preyed upon the gullibility of the people.

The Roman procurator in every case dealt with the charlatans. Thomas Newton observed that, "Many of them were apprehended and killed every day." Jesus said, "See that no one misleads you, for many will come in my name, saying 'I am the Christ,' and will mislead many." [11] As it was at the time of Jesus' first Advent, so shall it be during His Second Advent.

There are so many false Messiahs offering false hope in these perilous times.

Historically, there also has been another problem of sincere theologians who sincerely misinterpreted Biblical chronology. As we sift the wreckage of the past ages, there have been many doomsayers who were doomed to failure. It is much like the famous story of the shepherd boy and the wolf: when the wolf finally appeared in earnest, no one believed the shepherd boy, so no one came to the rescue.

On New Year's Eve, 999 A.D., Pope Sylvester II celebrated what he and many faithful thought would be the last midnight mass of history, believing that based on Revelation twenty verses seven and eight, the end of the world would occur when Satan would be bound for a thousand years. The whole of Christendom prepared for the final hour. This is how Russell Chandler encapsulated the events:

> "This was the final hour, the beginning of the day of wrath, the nightfall of the universe, the fateful and dreaded eve of the return of the millennium when the earth would dissolve into ashes. Outside, anxious crowds flooded the streets. Church bells rang out what most thought would not be a New Year, but history's finale. And in Jerusalem, thousands of pilgrims milled about hysterically, flocking to the spot where they expected Jesus to descend from the clouds. All across Europe, people gave away homes and goods to the poor as acts of contrition. Debts were forgiven, businesses closed, farms abandoned, fields left uncultivated, farm animals free to roam away, prisoners released, and masses seeking absolution. Flagellants roamed the countryside, whipping one another in penitence and mortification. "[1]

---

[1] Chandler, Russell (*"Doomsday: The End of the World--A View Through Time,"* 47-48).

On New Year's Eve, at St. Peters, Pope Sylvester II raised his hands skyward. The crowds, dressed in sackcloth and ashes remained transfixed, scarcely daring to breathe. Midnight came: there was a holy hush that seemed like eternity. The clock continued to tick into the New Year. Alas! It was the new millennium and nothing happened! The Ten Deum was sung. No fire fell from heaven. History is littered with such failed predictions about the end of the world.

It happened again with the Y2K events: unwary believers were caught up in another false millennium fever. Each generation has had its own end time predictions to no avail.

The doomsday clock featured in the Bulletin of Atomic Scientists magazine, in January 1981, has its hands moved to four minutes until midnight. The Mayan calendar puts earth's expiration date at December 21, 2012.

Setting dates for the end of the world is nothing new. There is a long tragic history of date setting for the end of the world. In the light of the horrible events we are going through, could it be that this is at last the real dateline? This book reveals earth's expiration date according to the book of Daniel. The date is near. Could it thus not be a coincidence that for the first time, earth is running out of everything vital for human survival?

For the first time in history, all the signs of the time converge, including biochip implants predicted in scripture, which never existed until now. Time will tell whether our decoded time matrix of Daniel's sealed message is correct or not. What history has taught us is not to abandon our short term and long term plans because of the nearness of the end time. God forbid!

The right response is not running away, as it will ruin you and your family. Run *with* God, because *the way out is up*. Historically date setters have lived doomed lives. When nothing happened after their set date passed, they gave up because they had lost everything and would have had to start over. But remember: the battle for the future is not human. The Word of God says, "for the battle is not yours, but God's." [12] The only right response is to brighten the corner where you are. The only thing to fear is fear itself.

This is the hour for preparation, to participate in your end time destiny, preordained before the foundation of the world. This is not time to run and hide, while burying your talent in the ground.

When Jesus knew that the Messianic Clock had arrived to the last day of His life, He did not quit. He put in a full day's work, and then had a party with His friends that evening! He didn't change anything— afterwards, He went, as usual, to His regular place of prayer. When you walk at the center of God's will, there is no need to change anything. Your future security comes from being at the center of God's will.

It is a fact: God wants His children to know the Messianic Clock, so when doomsday arrives, they are prepared to meet their God. He revealed it in His Word. He said it would be decoded in the last days. It is clear, precise and straightforward. This is the good news. The bad news is that previous date setters may have led some of God's people to become disillusioned, rather than prepared, for this critical time.

Historically, the failed misinterpretation has been based upon allegorical and figurative interpretation of clear scriptures. The Bible is written for simple people to understand. It is God's love letter, that was written to be understood by His children in a simple and straightforward way. The Word of God does not require fancy footnotes. It is literal.

The Messianic Clock is literal. When it says a virgin shall give birth, it simply means that, even though to the human mind, it seems impossible. When it says the Messiah will be cut off, it means exactly that. The Jews could not comprehend how the Messiah would be cut off and at the same time rule forever. Rationalistic interpretation of revelation always leads to false assumptions.

The Bible contains more than one thousand predictions; half of them have already been fulfilled, without fail, at the preset times on the Messianic Clock. Divine timeline is infallible. God's reputation rests upon the integrity of His Word.

The danger has been rationalists replacing the literal meaning of God's Word with an allegorical or figurative interpretation, in an attempt to make sense of the divine enigma. Dispensationalists try to fit their interpretations into their scheme and framework of things, to no avail.

Needless to say, we need not throw away the baby with the bath water, since Daniel wrote:

> "And he said, Go *your way*, Daniel, for the words *are* closed up and sealed till the time of the end. Many shall be purified, made white, and refined, but the wicked shall do wickedly; and none of the wicked shall understand, but the wise shall understand." [13]

The Apostle Paul, speaking about the time of the second coming of the Lord, said this about the saints living in those days:

> "But you, brothers and sisters, are *not in darkness so that this day should surprise you like a thief.* You are all children of the light and children of the day. We do not belong to the night or to the darkness." [14]

Daniel predicts that the wise will understand the enigma and will instruct many. The Apostle Paul says the saints will not be in darkness, that that day should "overtake them like a thief in the night." [15] The book of Revelation says:

> "The revelation from Jesus Christ, which God gave Him to show His servants what must soon take place. He made it known by sending His angel to His servant John, who testifies to everything he saw—that is, the Word of God and the testimony of Jesus Christ. Blessed is the one who reads aloud the words of this prophecy, and blessed are those who hear it and take to heart what is written in it, because the time is near." [16]

We have evidence of the infallibility of Biblical predictions and failed human interpretation. The many predictions that were fulfilled at the appointed time are the basis of our assuming that future predictions also will be fulfilled on time.

We debunk the myth that prophecy teaching is to be left alone, as Biblical end time prophecies cannot be deciphered. I encourage each reader to "prove all things; hold fast that which is good." [17]   I am not writing this book as a seer or a prophet, but as one who "sees through a glass darkly," and knows in part. Only the Word of God is infallible: "blessed are those who hear and take it to heart what is written in it, because time is near." [18]

DOOMSDAY CAN BE POSTPONED

God is the sole author of history His will is final. Biblical evidence exists that God postpones his judgment if His people repent and turn back to him.

> "If my people, which are called by my name, shall humble
> themselves, and pray, and seek my face, and turn from
> their wicked ways; then will I hear from heaven, and will
> forgive their sin, and will heal their land." [19]

We have historical precedents in which God postponed His judgment. The people of Nineveh repented and He postponed His judgment for 40 years. He spared that generation that repented. Abraham pleaded with God for the cities of Sodom and Gomorrah; "And he said, indeed now, I have taken it upon myself to speak to the Lord: Suppose twenty should be found there? So He said, I will not destroy it for the sake of twenty. Suppose there were five less than the fifty righteous; would you destroy all of the city for lack of five? So He said, If I find there forty-five, I will not destroy it." [20]

Though the Bible gives a specific and definitive date for the end of the age, yet it remains conditional to mankind's response to His warnings. This is consistent with His nature and loving kindness. He desires that all men might be saved. The inevitability of doomsday in our generation depends upon what the people called by His name will do.

Careful observation of scriptures clearly shows that God is not dogmatic regarding these judgments. From our vantage point in history we are confronted with numerous times, when God postponed His judgments, which gives us the encouragement. The inevitability of His wrath being poured out always depends upon the cup of iniquity being filled to the brim.

This constitutes a hope for this terminal generation to avoid filling the cup full. It has the last chance to repent and turn away from its evil ways. The earth is being defiled with the blood of 100 million innocent babies being aborted each year. Their blood cries out to God for justice. Though judgment is overdue it is never too late for God's grace if this generation repents and turn away from its evil ways God will heal our land.

King Josiah lived during the time when God was ready to pour out His wrath upon Israel, because of her rebellion. He repented and sought God's grace and mercy. God heard his prayers and postponed the judgment.

> "Thus says the LORD: 'Behold, I will bring calamity on this place and on its inhabitants, all the curses that are written in the book which they have read before the king of Judah, because they have forsaken Me and burned incense to other gods, that they might provoke Me to anger with all the works of their hands.
>
> Therefore my wrath will be poured out on this place, and not be quenched.' But as for the king of Judah, who sent you to inquire of the LORD, in this manner you shall speak to him, 'Thus says the LORD God of Israel: "*Concerning* the words which you have heard— because your heart was tender, and you humbled yourself before God when you heard His words against this place and against its inhabitants, and you humbled yourself before Me, and you tore your clothes and wept before Me, I also have heard

you," says the LORD. "Surely I will gather you to your fathers, and you shall be gathered to your grave in peace; and your eyes shall not see all the calamity which I will bring on this place and its inhabitants." [21] So they brought back word to the king.

King Zedekiah's generation hardened its heart and dismissed God's warnings. God executed his judgment upon that generation.

"He did evil in the sight of the LORD his God, *and* did not humble himself before Jeremiah the prophet, *who spoke* from the mouth of the LORD.

Moreover all the leaders of the priests and the people transgressed more and more, *according* to all the abominations of the nations, and defiled the house of the LORD, which He had consecrated in Jerusalem.

And the LORD God of their fathers sent *warnings* to them by His messengers, rising up early and sending *them,* because He had compassion on His people and on His dwelling place. But they mocked the messengers of God, despised His words, and scoffed at His prophets, until the wrath of the LORD arose against His people, till *there was* no remedy.

Therefore He brought against them the king of the Chaldeans, who killed their young men with the sword in the house of their sanctuary, and had no compassion on young man or virgin, on the aged or the weak; He gave *them* all into his hand to fulfill the word of the LORD by the mouth of Jeremiah, until the land had enjoyed her Sabbaths. As long as she lay desolate she kept Sabbath, to fulfill seventy years." [22]

The generation of Noah did not give heed to His warning of the coming judgment of God. They all perished in the flood. Jesus said as it was in the days of Noah so shall it be. The judgment was not postponed because they continued in their evil ways.

The fact that God conditions his judgment on man's response to His warnings give this generation wonderful hope for God to postpone His judgment and spare this terminal generation on condition we turn from our evil ways and repent of our sins.

We are living in the Laodiceans church age. The Lord has a very specific warning to our generation:

> "I know your works, that you are neither cold nor hot. I could wish you were cold or hot. So then, because you are lukewarm, and neither cold nor hot I will vomit you out of My mouth. Because you say, 'I am rich, have become wealthy, and have need of nothing'—and do not know that you are wretched, miserable, poor, blind, and naked— I counsel you to buy from Me gold refined in the fire, that you may be rich; and white garments, that you may be clothed, *that* the shame of your nakedness may not be revealed; and anoint your eyes with eye salve, that you may see. As many as I love, I rebuke and chasten. Therefore be zealous and repent.
> Behold, I stand at the door and knock. If anyone hears My voice and opens the door, I will come in to him and dine with him, and he with Me. To him who overcomes I will grant to sit with Me on My throne, as I also overcame and sat down with My Father on His throne. "He who has an ear, let him hear what the Spirit says to the churches." [23]

Prophets for profit that run His church today have run Jesus out of His church. He is going knocking on the door of the heart from person to person outside His church. From this point forward the future of this generation depends upon the condition of men's hearts as they hear God's final warnings.

God is willing to forgive and give mankind many generations. The streams of His love never dry up, the fountain of His grace never fails, the sun of His righteousness never sets and the shield of His protection is never broken.

"Perhaps everyone will listen and turn from his evil way, that I may relent concerning the calamity which I purpose to bring on them because of the evil of their doings." [24]

The theologian Kierkegaard said, "Life must be lived forward but only understood backward." This terminal generation must live forward towards its approaching appointment with destiny, while praying for postponement of judgment understood backward in God's previous dealings with mankind. Mercy was obtained through repentance. Will this generation repent?

The thing that concerns me the most is the fact that the spiritual condition predicted by the Apostle Paul to prevail in the last days exists today.

"Now, brethren, concerning the coming of our Lord Jesus Christ and our gathering together to Him, we ask you, not to be soon shaken in mind or troubled, either by spirit or by word or by letter, as if from us, as though the day of Christ had come. Let no one deceive you by any means; for that Day will not come unless the falling away comes first, and the man of sin is revealed, the son of perdition." [25]

The falling away of the believers is taking place right now. We have churches full of the chosen frozen, with a form of godliness without power. The church has been turned into big business and a social club. Though it seems too late it is never too late for God's grace if the people who are called by His name will humble themselves and repent and turn away from their evil ways. There is still hope for the elect of God. "They will overcome the world by the blood of the lamb by the word of their testimony because they love not their lives unto death." [26]

CHAPTER ONE

THE PROPHETIC SIGN POSTS

The course of history has been planned from the dawn of time. Earth days are numbered and revealed in Bible prophecy. The scriptures give us clear future profiles of the ages, from the outset of time to the end of days. History has chronicled world events in the last 6000 years in perfect harmony with the prophetic timeline, with absolutely no inconsistencies. Human destiny is not a matter of chance. There is no controversy in the fact that everything in history has been preordained and the dateline preset.

Today however, in a supreme irony, there are still skeptics who doubt God's Word, in spite of such undeniable evidence. One has only to consider that no human analysis and prognostication can foretell the events 6,000 years ahead.

The scope and magnitude of Biblical prophecies makes it indisputable that God inspired the writers. History is in the hands of God. It cannot be emphasized enough that according to the Messianic clock, these are the final days on earth, based upon a proven history of infallibility.

In our journey from the dawn of time to the new heaven and new earth, God has posted some signposts along the highway of time. These signs of the time tell mankind what to expect.

There is for the first time in history a perfect correlation between the signs of the time and the encoded timeline in His Word. All through history, God provides His children details for the coming events and the exact calendar to expect them. Peter was able to say on the day of Pentecost, "This is that which was spoken by the prophet Joel." [27]

The disciples asked Jesus, "Tell us, when will this happen and what will be the sign of your coming and of the end of the ages?" Jesus said, "Even so, when you see these things (signs of the time), you know that it is near, right at the door. I tell you the truth, this generation will certainly not pass away until these things have happened." [28] Jesus gave the backdrop events to look for. Daniel gives scheduled events and the dateline to make sure that the saints would know what to expect in each generation.

THE CURRENT SIGNS OF THE TIME CONFIRM
THE MESSIANIC CLOCK TO DOOMSDAY

The issue before us is this: do the current events support the validity that these are the last days? Are we seeing the signs Jesus said to look for? The answer is that our current events are a fulfillment of Biblical prophecy. For the first time, it is an undeniable fact that the end signs of time are happening so rapidly and in such variety that words are inadequate to describe their terrifying speed.

The forces that are changing our generation are ominous. There is intensified acceleration. It is hard to doubt that this is the terminal generation, as foretold by the ancient prophets.

This is not the hour for irrational exuberance; we are in a predicament that precedes the death of western civilization. The stimulus packages have failed; the global economy is shattered. We are seeing for the first time the specter of global economic collapse and unsustainable deficits. Over-leveraged corporations are cutting jobs, causing unprecedented massive global unemployment and whole industries being destroyed. Looming in the wings is the collapse of nation states, law and order, and western civilization itself.

The present crisis is beyond the scope of market bulls and bears. Systems are in terminal crisis. What should be clear is that the meltdown is a powder keg about to blow, and the fuse is lit. We have already seen various edifices of our civilization collapsing and sending global shock waves. There is panic on Wall Street and Main Street because, contrary to what the "pundits" say, we have not been this way before.

THE FUTURE HAS BEEN PRERECORDED

What you may not know is that everything happening has been predicted with startling details 2,500 years ago. All the signs given in Biblical prophecy of the end of earth time are verifiable today in our world. The last days of earth history are slipping away while mankind is bedazzled by the last decades sizzled and fizzled global economy. This generation is beleaguered and distraught over what is happening. "One hundred cities in America and 46 states are bankrupt. The FDIC, which insures 13 trillion dollars in deposits, is 21 billion dollars in the hole." [2]

The unthinkable and unimaginable is happening: a phantom economy, based upon a phantom dollar created out of thin air, has become the basis of our economy. The world is falling apart—everything is unraveling. There is mounting evidence that this is the terminal generation.

Daniel was given a precise calendar of the end time events. The Bible has a lot to say about our times. Biblical prophecy is a guide for sorting it all out. What is startling is perhaps the transparency across the spectrum of how ancient predictions are visibly playing out in our world today. Present events that on the surface appear as uncertain, unsettling, upsetting and confusing are all explained in these ancient predictions being fulfilled before our very eyes. You can know what time it is by looking at the prophetic signposts.

THIS IS THE TERMINAL GENERATION

Unfortunately, centuries of reckless, speculative interpretations that proved false have turned many away from Biblical prophecy. Some modern scholars spiritualize and marginalize literal fulfillment of prophecy, while most secular intellectuals regard it as a myth. Mainline Christianity looks at it as meaningless symbolism, and to their peril, the mainstream of society views prophecy as fiction.

It is easy to understand why people are turned off, since American spiritual spectrums are dominated by falsehoods, immorality, seduction and bizarre delusions that have put this generation into a spiritual stupor. There is no clear prophetic voice. The prophet Daniel predicted that in the end of days, the wicked would not understand. I believe it is because

---

[2] (http://www.investmentu.com/2010/February/the-fdic-twenty-billion-problem.html).

of too much confusion in the church. How can a lost church that itself does not know what time it is, warn this terminal generation?

The hour of destiny has come, preset by God. History is not random: it is designed, and a time framework established from creation. There can be no mistake that history follows a predetermined Messianic Clock, revealed in scriptures from antiquity to doomsday.

Throughout history, God has given mankind the Messianic clock for all divine visitations until the end of time. There are no coincidences in history. Every event fits perfectly with God's larger design of the ages laid out beforehand in the scriptures.

We have startling revelations and documented evidence of the infallibility of the scriptures. These lead to certainty beyond any reasonable doubt that we are in the last days. The time on the Messianic clock is nearing zero hour.

As we are drawing near to the grand finale and climactic close of the ages, this book is written to provide you with a Biblical perspective of our immediate future in this decade of destiny. By sharing with you the exquisite and precise dateline, which God encoded in His Holy Word regarding your approaching appointment with destiny, it is my prayer that you will make peace with God.

Do not follow the crowd, since this generation is woefully and tragically ignorant of its destiny. There is an undeniable parallel between this generation and Noah's pre-flood generation, which rejected God's warning. We are already experiencing the tremors and momentous end-of-days shockwaves beginning to erupt on every side, yet we are so desensitized to evil that we ignore the obvious signs.

It won't be long before God replaces this chaotic order with beauty and harmony. The earth will be restored to its former glory, tranquility, blessedness and righteousness. There will soon be no more sorrow or pain, for the former things will pass away. We stand at the dawn of a glorious new day.

Every day, new evidences keep mounting to show our generation is on the brink of the end of the present order of things. The wisest man ever to live, Solomon, said, "A wise man's heart discerns both time and judgment." [29] It is time for us to do so.

IT IS CRITICAL TO KNOW THE FUTURE

Why should anyone be interested in the future? Famous American inventor Charles Kettering once said, "I am interested in the future because that's where I am going to spend the remainder of my life."[3] Biblical prophecy gives you a preview of tomorrow, so you can prepare for it, because that's where you are going to spend your eternal future.

Biblical prophecy is indispensable for your survival. Study God's Word and believe its predictions. It is God's road map to guide you through the impending and overwhelming catastrophe of the "end game." Prophecy will dispel the bewilderment of the horrific events that wait this generation. We are now approaching a critical juncture, as eternity intercepts time.

Jesus specifically said regarding this terminal generation, "Men's hearts failing them for fear, and for looking after those things which are coming on the earth: for the powers of heaven shall be shaken." [30]

Our civilization is rapidly speeding toward the precipice, while mankind remains hopeless, impotent and overwhelmed with economic meltdown and unprecedented natural disasters. The world wants everyone to believe that the natural catastrophe is a result of man-made climate change. God preset these signs from the foundation of the world: signs of the end of earth days.

Every headline in the global village is aligning with ancient prophecies and assuming more and more Biblical characteristics. It is becoming very hard to relegate these predictions as folklore. We are watching the stage being set right on schedule for the endgame, in our lifetime as predicted, yet hardly anyone is warning this terminal generation.

Unfortunately while prophecy is being fulfilled before our very eyes, the chilling reality is that scientific opinion has tragically acclimatized

---

[3] Walvoord, John F., 'Armageddon, Oil and Terror' (Tyndale, 2007 ed.)p.l.

people to dismiss Biblical prophecy as irrelevant, during this most critical hour in history. It is great folly to trivialize, marginalize, ignore and discard the prophetic as delusional. It is God's warning to his people. The hard skeptic sees Biblical fundamentalism as a threat to progress and global peace.

God will not change His definitive timeline and specific deadline for the end of the world just because this generation buries its head in the sand like an ostrich. It is time to run for your dear life, since it will soon be too late.

God has given us detailed information and signs to watch for. The date is specific and the details are becoming clearer as they are being fulfilled daily in our very sight. There is no ambiguity in God's Word. The hour is late and mankind's appointment with God is upon us in just a few years, according to the Daniel time matrix. In spite of the fact that we are ignoring the signs of the times, as forecasted thousands of years ago, it will not change the fact that the present scheme of things is soon coming to an end.

Our present generation is dominated with pride and greed, and chooses to ignore God's Word as irrelevant, and as a crutch for the simple and uneducated.

The Bible identifies the forces of Islam as the cause of the final battle on earth. The Islamic conflict has already begun, and will consummate in the final holocaust against Israel. The confrontation has already begun. It is time for the believers to look up with joy for the blessed return of Jesus Christ to set up His Kingdom on this planet. The tempo is picking up. We have already passed the point of no return. The trajectory is irreversible and final. The end of all things is here. The question is, are you ready?

THIS IS THE HOUR FOR PREPARATION

The present world order is growing more and more oppressive, pervasive and impersonal. Human autonomy and human rights are threatened more every day. Everything happening in our generation is a sign of the end of days, as forecasted in antiquity. "This generation shall not pass, till all these things be fulfilled." [31] God wants his children to read the writing on the Wall Street and on Main Street.

Together we will marshal all the scriptures and decode the time matrix concealed in the sacred literature from ages past. We will see how Daniel's sealed message interprets the events of our time.

The message is encoded in the Old Testament and decoded in the New Testament. The wise will understand, but the wicked will not understand. They will mock the inerrant and infallible Word of God. This was clearly predicted in Peter's writings 2,000 years ago, when the Spirit of God projected him into our day. This is how he describes our terminal generation:

> "Knowing this first, that there shall come in the last days scoffers, walking after their own lusts, and saying, "Where is the promise of His coming?" For since the fathers fell asleep, all things continue as they were from the beginning of the creation. For this they willingly are ignorant of, that by the Word of God, the heavens were of old, and the earth standing out of the water and in the water;
>
> Whereby the world that then was, being overflowed with water, perished; but the heavens and the earth, which are now, by the same word are kept in store, reserved unto fire against the Day of Judgment and perdition of ungodly men. But, beloved, be not ignorant of this one thing: that one-day is with the Lord as a thousand years, and a thousand years as one day.
>
> The Lord is not slack concerning His promise, as some men count slackness; but is longsuffering to us-ward, not willing that any should perish, but that all should come to repentance. But the Day of the Lord will come as a thief in the night; in which the heavens shall pass away with a great noise, and the elements shall melt with fervent heat, the earth also, and the works that are therein shall be burned up.

Seeing then that all these things shall be dissolved, what manner of person ought ye to be in all holy conversation and godliness, looking for and hastening unto the coming of the Day of God, wherein the heavens being on fire shall melt with fervent heat? Nevertheless we, according to His promise, look for new heavens and a new earth, in which righteousness dwells." [32]

Moral decay and spiritual erosion in our world today are pointing to the eminence of the last days and the end of time in our lifetime. We are witnessing the scoffers walking after their own lusts.

Biblical prophecy enables us to identify and understand the factors that are shaping tomorrow's headlines. Since precision timing is essential to God's revealed master plan of the ages, we do well to pay attention to Biblical prophecy datelines concerning our generation.

What is God's plan for this generation? He wants you to prepare for the end of days like Noah did. Our generation is at the threshold of the New World and paradise restored. We have entered the twilight zone and are fast approaching zero hour. We are now in the critical stage foreshadowed in the end time prophecies of a time of great distresses.

Jesus' first Advent was foretold, and it happened exactly at the pre-set time revealed in the Holy Scriptures. The second coming of Jesus will also happen at the revealed time in His Word. Jesus said, "I have told you all things." [33] "All things *mean* all things." All the pieces of the puzzle have been revealed. The timeline, the sequence of future events, and the players of the end game are all revealed. God gives us detailed information, a precise timetable, from Paradise lose to Paradise restored: the new Heaven and the new Earth.

It is time to build an Ark. If you do not prepare now, what you fear will come upon you. In the past, we have had gloom and boom. The next gloom will lead to doom. We have seen many signs of the things to come: market volatility, corporate meltdowns, financial market upheaval, credit markets bursting, and global economic convulsions. These are the rumblings of an approaching hurricane, whose eye is still out at sea. The storm may seem like it has weakened, only to gather greater destructive strength. This is the perfect storm of the ages. Build your house on the Rock of Ages.

NASA WARNING OF THE APPROACHING INTERSTELLAR STORM

One of the major signs of the times will be in space. Jesus predicted that before the end of the world there will be signs in the sky.

> "And there will be great earthquakes in various places, and famines and pestilences; and there will be fearful sights and great signs from heaven.
> And there will be signs in the sun, in the moon, and in the stars; and on the earth distress of nations, with perplexity, the sea and the waves roaring; men's hearts failing them from fear and the expectation of those things which are coming on the earth, for the powers of the heavens will be shaken." [34]

NASA and the European Space Agency are warning the world of a once in a lifetime super interstellar storm. NASA warns that killer Solar Flares could threaten life on earth in this decade. Our planet is passing through a highly electrified cloud of gas, everything in our Solar System is heading into alien unknown photon cloud, a belt of danger that could precipitate gigantic solar explosion, magnetic anomalies, careering cometary masses and destabilizing the orbits of some asteroids.

The bottom line is we are heading towards more frequent solar storm and coronal mass ejections (cmes) super massive flares that will threaten our planet with deadly radioactive baths. Jesus said, "men's hearts failing them for fear and looking after those things which are coming on the earth, for the powers of the heavens shall be shaken." [35]

The scientific world is terrified at the signs of things they see coming towards us out of space. They are predicting major climate change, massive earthquakes, volcanic activity, tsunamis and even an ice age. These are the signs that Jesus spoke about before the end of the age. He said the generation that will witness the rebirth of Israel and the revival of the Roman Empire, as the European Community will not pass away. Israel was reborn in 1948. The Treaty of Rome revived the Roman Empire in 1957. Ours is the blessed generation that will see the coming of the Lord.

THE DAY OF THE RAPTURE IS NOT KNOWN

Jesus told His disciples that the day and hour of his coming is not revealed. Only God the Father knows it.

> "But of that day and hour no one knows, not even the angels in heaven, nor the Son, but only the Father." [36]

Equally important is the fact that He never said, no man will know the time of the end of the age or end of the world since the rapture takes place first, and no man knows the day or hour. Nevertheless Jesus went ahead and told his disciples the exact sign for the end of the world:

> "Now learn this parable from the fig tree: When its branch has already become tender and puts forth leaves, you know that summer *is* near. So you also, when you see all these things, know that it is near—at the doors! Assuredly, I say to you, this generation will by no means pass away till all these things take place. Heaven and earth will pass away, but My words will by no means pass away." [37]

Jesus pinpoints when the world will end. The generation that witnesses the rebirth of Israel and the Roman Empire will see the end of the world. The generation from the rebirth of Israel and the Roman Empire can be calculated. This reveals when the world will end.

Daniel was given a specific termination date for the world. John in the book of Revelation explains it. Jesus clearly revealed the time of the end of the world. This date is revealed in scripture. It is the end of the generation that witnessed these momentous events. We are living in the terminal generation and in the final days.

The disciples asked Jesus to reveal to them the timeline for three major events regarding future.

> "Now as He sat on the Mount of Olives, the disciples came to Him privately, saying, "Tell us, when will these things be? And what *will be* the sign of your coming, and of the end of the age?" [38]

The first question had to do with the destruction of the Temple. He gave them a very specific answer. The numerical value of what he said revealed the year 70 A.D. for the destruction of the Temple. This is the reason why all the believers left Jerusalem before Titus destroyed it. Josephus wrote that not one Christian was found in the city. They knew when Jerusalem was going to be destroyed.

The second question was about the rapture of the saints. He gave them signs to look for, very specific to be able to tell every saint the nearness of His coming. All the prime clues were given and actual events up to the minute, to the degree that Jesus told them, "Behold I have told you all things." [39]

SIGNS OF THE RAPTURE

Here is how Jesus encapsulated the signs of his coming:

> "And Jesus answered and said unto them, Take heed that no man deceive you. For many shall come in my name, saying, I am Christ; and shall deceive many. And ye shall hear of wars and rumors of wars: see that ye be not troubled: for all these things must come to pass, but the end is not yet.
> For nation shall rise against nation, and kingdom against kingdom: and there shall be famines, and pestilences, and earthquakes, in diverse places. All these are the beginning

of sorrows. Then shall they deliver you up to be afflicted, and shall kill you: and ye shall be hated of all nations for my name's sake. And then shall many be offended, and shall betray one another, and shall hate one another. And many false prophets shall rise, and shall deceive many. And because iniquity shall abound, the love of many shall wax cold.

But he that shall endure unto the end, the same shall be saved. And this gospel of the kingdom shall be preached in all the world for a witness unto all nations; and then shall the end come. When ye therefore shall see the abomination of desolation, spoken of by Daniel the prophet, stand in the holy place, (whoso reads, let him understand:)" "So likewise ye, when ye shall see all these things, know that it is near, even at the doors. Verily I say unto you, this generation shall not pass, till all these things be fulfilled. Heaven and earth shall pass away, but my words shall not pass away." [40]

We are living in the days, when the world is on a fast track towards fulfilling all the signs of the times foretold by the Lord Jesus. The global trends we are witnessing in this direction are shocking in suddenness and scope. The world has gone beyond the point of no return.

A firm grasp of how current headlines, the Bible and end time prophecies fit together, constitute the reason the whole world is talking about the end of the world. The Biblical predictions of the end of time long scoffed and ridiculed are suddenly taking center stage across a shattered world.

There are over one thousand predictions in the Bible regarding the first and second coming of Christ. Biblical prophecy envisions the rise of a cashless society, social upheaval, global nuclear holocaust, biometric implant with the number 666, one world government of the Antichrist, one world religion of the false prophet, counterfeit Christs, one world economy, the apostasy of the church, global food shortage, ethnic cleansing, global financial collapse, societal moral decay, collapse of nation states, lawlessness, tribulation of the saints and attempted extermination of the Jews. Jesus said, "so likewise you when you shall see all these things know that it is near, even at the door." [41]

We are seeing all the signs of the time foretold in the Bible. For that reason I believe the Antichrist is alive and well in the world today. There are ever increasing signs in our present day that seem to clearly indicate behind the scenes stage-setting that precede the full fledge rise of the One World Order ruled by the Antichrist. It's becoming more and more easy to see how all these pieces of the puzzle are beginning to fall in place.

It's now possible to construct the big picture of our immediate future consistent with the Biblical outlook of the last days, since all the pieces of the puzzle regarding the rapture, are all available for the first time in human history. From this time on it is hard to envision anyone doubting the infallibility of Biblical prophecy.

The message of these ancient predictions is imperative to every human being alive today as it relates to the immediate ultimate destiny of all mankind. What's more Jesus is the only hope. No one can afford to miss accepting Jesus as Lord and Savior in this hour.

Now the question remains what did Jesus say are the signs of the end of the age? First we must define what the end of the age means. There are three Biblical ages or dispensations, the Age of Conscience from Adam to Abraham, the Age of the Law from Abraham to Jesus first Advent, the Age of the Church from the baptism of Jesus to his second coming, each age is exactly two thousand years.

The Rapture ends the age of the church and ushers in the age of the Kingdom. The Rapture is the end of the dispensation of grace. During the Rapture the saints will be caught up to meet the Lord in the air for the Wedding Feast of the Lamb, the Bema judgment seat of Christ, to receive the rewards and return with Christ to set up the millennium kingdom.

THE TERMS THAT THE NEW TESTAMENT USES
TO DESCRIBE THE RAPTURE

Parousia	to arrive in a visible, bodily form	For what *is* our hope, or joy, or crown of rejoicing? *Is it* not even you in the presence of our Lord Jesus Christ at His coming? 1 Thessalonians 2:19
Katabiono	to come down or descend	For the Lord Himself will descend from heaven with a shout, with the voice of an archangel, and with the trumpet of God. And the dead in Christ will rise first. 1 Thessalonians 4:16
Apokalupsis	to unveil or uncover his appearing	and to give you who are troubled rest with us when the Lord Jesus is revealed from heaven with His mighty angels. 2 Thessalonians 1 :7
Phaneroo	To appear or manifest	Beloved, now we are children of God; and it has not yet been revealed what we shall be, but we know that when He is revealed, we shall be like Him, for we shall see Him as He is. 1 John 3:2
Epiphaino	The appearance of his brightness at His coming	And then the lawless one will be revealed, whom the Lord will consume with the breath of His mouth and destroy with the brightness of His coming. 2 Thessalonians 2:8
Erchomai	The act of coming	Then the sign of the Son of Man will appear in heaven, and then all the tribes of the earth will mourn, and they will see the Son of Man coming on the clouds of heaven with power and great glory. Matthew 24:30
Horao	To see with the eyes or to appear visibly	so Christ was offered once to bear the sins of many. To those who eagerly wait for Him He will appear a second time, apart from sin, for salvation. Hebrews 9:28
Episunagoges	To be gathered unto him	For you yourselves know, brethren, that our coming to you was not in vain. 1 Thessalonians 2:1
Harpazo	To be snatched away at His coming	Then we who are alive *and* remain shall be caught up together with them in the clouds to meet the Lord in the air. And thus we shall always be with the Lord. 1 Thessalonians 4:17

CHAPTER TWO

MESSIANIC CLOCK: THE PROPHETIC TIME MAPS

The drama our generation is engaged in has been written from eternity past, before the foundation of the world. God is the playwright. The script is written and recorded in the bible. It is clear, exact, and the timeline precise. The prophets were given a preview of the events from His vantage point, looking down the corridor of time, backward and forward to the end of days. God gave them the calendar of the ages.

The prophets predicted the events and pinpointed the timing preset by God before the foundation of the world, for each prophetic event until doomsday.

It is important to keep in mind that from the dawn of time, God is a date setter. Historical precedent reveals the indisputable conclusion that God has always kept His appointments He had His prophets predict. He is an on time God. He never missed His divine appointments with mankind.

The correlation of biblical prophecies and the corresponding historical events reveals the infallibility of God's declared timing. God reveals the timetable of all future events. He always tells man the preset time. Not one prediction failed to happen according to the prophetic time map:

God told Noah the timeline until the flood would be <u>120 years.</u>

> "And the Lord said, 'My spirit shall not always strive with man, for that he also is flesh; yet his days shall be a hundred and twenty years." [42]

God told Abraham that his children would be in Egypt <u>400 years</u>.

> "And He said unto Abram, 'Know of a surety that thy seed shall be a stranger in a land that is not theirs, and shall serve them; and they shall afflict them four hundred years." [43]

God told Moses that the children of Israel would wander in the wilderness 40 years.

> "And your children shall wander in the wilderness 40 years, and bear your whoredoms, until your carcasses be wasted in the wilderness." [44]

Jeremiah was told Israel would be in Babylonian captivity 70 years.

> "For thus says the LORD: 'after seventy years are completed at Babylon, I will visit you and perform My good word toward you, and cause you to return to this place." [45]

It is not difficult to see that God has always told His people the exact time; contrary to widespread teaching that nobody will know when the next prophetic event will take place. God always gives a precise, exact timetable to every prophetic event.

It is a terrible tragedy to remain ignorant by choice, as the consequences are perilous. Modern Christianity has dismissed as irrelevant the Biblical calendar to doomsday, because of past erroneous predictions, false theology, misleading and fanciful speculations, and foolish forecasts that did not come to pass.

This revelation was reserved for the last days and for this generation. God said it would be revealed to the wise, and that the wise will understand the enigma and instruct many. [46] Biblical prophecy has never failed, but men's interpretations have. History bears witness that God's calendar is always accurate and infallible.

Daniel was told the Messiah would be cut off (crucified) 483 years from the decree by Cyrus to restore Jerusalem.

> "Know therefore and understand, that from the going forth of the command to restore and build Jerusalem, until Messiah the Prince, there shall be seven weeks and sixty-two weeks. The street shall be built again, and the wall

even in troublesome times. And after the sixty-two weeks Messiah shall be cut off, but not for Himself." [47]

It happened exactly as predicted, in 30 A.D., when Jesus was crucified, 483 years from Cyrus' decree to restore Jerusalem. Biblical timing is precision timing. God is a date setter.

It is important to point out that the Messianic Clock predicted the rise of all the world empires: from Egypt, Assyria, Babylon, Medo-Persia, Greece, Rome and the New World Order, in perfect sequence and duration until doomsday. Only a fool can doubt the infallibility of biblical prophecy.

MODERN DAY TIME MAP EVENTS

In the 20th Century, a Messianic Clock prediction was fulfilled upon the rebirth of the modern state of Israel in 1948. God said, "For behold, the days are coming,' says the LORD, 'that I will bring back from captivity My people Israel and Judah,' says the LORD. 'And I will cause them to return to the land that I gave to their fathers, and they shall possess it." [48]

The Bible predicted the revival of Rome, which we now know as the European Community. Also, the former USSR collapsed for denying the Jews exit visas to return to their ancient homeland as the preset time on the Messianic Clock had approached. God said, "I will say to the north, Give up, and to the south, Keep not back. Bring My sons from afar, and my daughters from the ends of the earth." [49]

The USSR failed to heed God's command to "Give up" and let the Jews go, as their appointed time had come to return, according to the preset time on the Messianic clock. God collapsed the USSR to set the Jews free to go, just as He did to Egypt.

In 1517 the Ottoman Empire took Jerusalem, and in 1917, exactly four hundred years later, the first Light Horse Brigade from British ally Australia, liberated Palestine. Fifty years later, in the Biblically significant Jubilee year of 1967, Temple Mount was returned to its rightful owners in the Six-Day War. This is divinely precise timing. Property must be restored to its rightful owners in the 50th year — Year of Jubilee. Five million Jews defeated 300 million Arabs in just six days a clear divine intervention.

DROUGHT CONDITIONS FOR FOREIGN
OCCUPIERS OF THE HOLY LAND PREDICTED

When the Jews returned in 1948 the desert blossomed. God kept his promise for nearly two thousand years the land was a desert wasteland, barren and unproductive landscape until the rightful heirs returned.

God promised that the Holy Land would become a desolate wasteland difficult to survive in for the foreigners occupying the land when He banishes Israel from the land. "I will make the land so desolate and your enemies who dwell upon it will be totally unproductive." [50] For one thousand five hundred years the Promised Land blossomed when the Jews were living in it. After Titus destroyed Jerusalem and exiled the Jews, the land became desolate for one thousand eight hundred years. Mark Twain in 1860 wrote this about his observation during his visit to Palestine. "The further we went (towards Jerusalem) the hotter the sun got and rockier and barren, repulsive and dreary the landscape became. There was hardly a tree or shrub anywhere. I would not desire to live there. It is a hopeless, dreary, heartbroken land. Palestine sits in sackcloth and ashes." [4]

THE DESTRUCTION OF IRAQ (ANCIENT BABYLON) BY
"OPERATION DESERT STORM" AND "THE COALITION OF THE WILLING"
WAS PREDICTED 2,500 YEARS AGO

The Prophet Jeremiah predicted two destructions of Babylon, "Then it will come to pass, when seventy years are completed, that I will punish the King of Babylon and that nation, the land of the Chaldeans, for their iniquity, thus says the Lord" [51] The first destruction was by the Medo-Persians in 539 B.C. The second destruction was predicted to happen in the distant future in two phases. The first will be "Desert Storm" which

---

[4] Prophecies For The Era of Muslim Terror, A Torah Perspective on World Events by Rabbi Menachem Kohen

the prophet Jeremiah called "A destroying wind" [52] and the second phase by the "Coalition of the Willing", which Jeremiah calls "an assembly of great nations". [53] Both destructions happened as predicted after 70 years from its rising as a nation. The second destruction was predicted to be through a coalition of nations. The prophesy is very specific: "For behold I am arousing and raising up against Babylon (modern day Iraq) a coalition of great nations…. They will array themselves for battle against her from there she will be captured. His arrows are like a smart conqueror, they shall not return empty-handed (smart bombs)." [54]

The prophecy concerning the fall of modern day Babylon clearly and accurately foretold that the first military operation would be called "Desert Storm." President George Bush Senior called his military campaign "Desert Storm." The second military campaign was by President George Bush Junior, which led to the final fall of Babylon was called a "Coalition of the Willing." The prophecy was accurate and definitive and specific. The modern Babylon was destroyed immediately after its seventieth anniversary as foretold of old.

DESCRIPTION OF A MODERN AIR FORCE 2500 YEARS AGO

Jeremiah, the prophet, was projected into the distant future by the Holy Spirit and saw a modern air show. He gives us startling and amazing description of the modern air force. This is his vivid picture of what he saw: "They come up as clouds… and chariots… as whirlwinds, swifter than eagles." [55] This is an impeccable description of our modern day air force. This is indisputable evidence that verifies biblical prophecy beyond any shadow of doubt. We are witnessing the fulfillment of ancient prophecy in an astoundingly breathtaking and earth shattering way.

PARTITIONING OF THE HOLY LAND BY THE
GENERAL ASSEMBLY OF THE UNITED NATIONS IN 1947

Here is more irrefutable evidence of amazing patterns of predictable constancy and occurrence of Biblical prophecy in our modern times. The prophet, Joel, foretold that the General Assembly of the United Nations will partition the Holy Land in the distant future before the advent of the

Messiah. The idea of all the nations agreeing to partition the Holy Land was unfathomable 2,500 years ago. He describes Resolution 181 and 242, to partition the Holy Land, and its final consequences from the covenant keeping God:

> "For behold, in those days and at that time, when I bring
> back the captives of Judah and Jerusalem, I will also gather
> all nations, and bring them down to the Valley of
> Jehoshaphat; And I will enter into judgment with them
> there on account of My people, My heritage Israel, whom
> they have scattered among the nations; They have also
> divided up My land."[56]

God says He will judge all nations because all the nations participated in the passing of the resolutions to partition His land.

THE BODY OF HITLER WILL NOT BE FOUND

The prophet, Daniel, describes the end of Hitler, the butcher of six million Jews with such details of an eyewitness: His retreat and final fall and what happened to his body. "He shall turn his face towards the fort of his own land: but he shall stumble and fall and not be found."[57] The body of Hitler has never been found. Daniel tells us his body will never be found.

God ordained the defeat of Hitler. He foretold his end. The allies were used as an instrument of God to execute judgment on the axis of evil. As Hitler retreated he stumbled and fell and his body will never be found.

AGE OF GLOBAL AND SPACE TRAVEL

Perhaps the most surprising sign of the times predicted 2,500 years ago is global and space travel; "many shall run to and fro."[58] What was once thought impossible in ancient time until recently "running to and fro at the speed of sound." Many dreamed of traveling into outer space and thought it impossible yet today man has walked on the moon and built a space station. We are living in the most incredible times the world has ever known. Mankind is now exploring the possibility of traveling to distant planets.

Earth travel, which used to take many months to travel by boat, now takes hours to go round the globe at the speed of sound. Hundreds of thousands of people run to and fro by air to distant places each day. Just in America alone there are 87,000 flights a day. This is the vision that Daniel saw of a generation coming in the last days that will run to and fro. We are a generation on the go. This is an indisputable fulfillment of Daniel's prediction concerning the last days. The ultimate future that he saw in the distant future is here.

AGE OF KNOWLEDGE EXPLOSION

One of the most startling prophecies about the terminal generation is the information super highways and knowledge explosion, "knowledge will increase." [59] The universal access to wireless Internet anywhere on earth is fueling this information overload unprecedented in history.

This global communication wave is making news available in real time as it is happening anywhere in the world. This is the most informed generation. Information is being transmitted at the speed of light from one end of the globe to another. We are living in an age when Daniel's prophecy is being fulfilled. History is verifying the accuracy of his prediction concerning our cyber space generation.

UNPRECEDENTED MORAL EROSION
AS A SIGN OF THE END OF DAYS

Jesus said, "As it was in the days of Noah so shall it be." [60] "The wickedness of man was great on the earth and that every intent of man's heart was only evil continually." [61] The moral condition that existed in the day of Noah is prevalent in the world today. The apostle Paul gives vivid predictions of the moral conditions in the last days:

> "But know this, that in the last days perilous times will come: For men will be lovers of themselves, lovers of money, boasters, proud, blasphemers, disobedient to

parents, unthankful, unholy, unloving, unforgiving, slanderers, without self-control, brutal, despisers of good, traitors, headstrong, haughty, lovers of pleasure rather than lovers of God, having a form of godliness but denying its power. And from such people turn away! For of this sort are those who creep into households and make captives of gullible women loaded down with sins, led away by various lusts always learning and never able to come to the knowledge of the truth." [62]

This present generation is characterized by a tidal wave of moral erosion, excessive evil has been uncorked, unimaginable sexual perversion and homosexuality, shameful debauchery, same sex marriage, shocking child pornography and child sacrifice, rampant drug addiction, mind-boggling scale of abortion on demand, human trafficking, overwhelming rate of violent crime, homicide and global terrorism, fixation on fantasy sexual sitcoms and entertainment, alarming increase of alcoholism and abuse of prescription drugs, sickening proliferation of corporate corruption and exploitation of the poor, government abuse of power, loss of individual rights and injustice.

There is a rise of paganism and godless humanism and new age religion. The morality of our present generation cannot be compared by any except that of the days of Noah. The judgment of God is inevitable. The world is going in the wrong direction with no one warning it.

The church is in a terrible malaise stripped of spiritual and moral authority by its spiritual paralysis. The church is depraved, delusional, decapacitated and defeated. It has become the whore of Babylon sleeping with every political beast, the mother of all harlots. The church has been turned into a social club, dominated by excessive immorality.

There is no difference between church marriages and secular, since more Christian marriages end up in divorce, a clear indictment on failed church leadership.

The church has maintained the form of godliness without reality, expression without manifestation, declaration without demonstration.

The majority of Christians are desensitized to sin. "Politically correct" is the new norm, and "feel good" social gospel, of happiness without holiness. The church has become apostate.

The moral conditions foretold to prevail at the end of the age exist in our present generation. It is impossible to entertain the thought that this is not the generation. The prophecy is remarkably precise, the language is literal, the description is clear, we are the generation. The present moral erosion and total depravity signify this generation's defiance of God.

Biblical prophecy is impeccable, accurate and literal. This generation is intoxicated with sin as predicted of old.

CHAPTER THREE

THE MESSIANIC CLOCK: LOST AND REPLACED BY
THE HISTORICAL CALENDAR DISTORTIONS

By far the most critical component for determining when doomsday will occur is to decode the date of creation, the date when time began. This is the crux of the matter--the tantalizing enigma, the concealed data. The scriptures establish the fact that mankind from time immemorial knew that the time span for this present order of things would elapse in 6000 years.

The question is, why all the confusion if this was known from the beginning? On the surface, it looks easy. There is nothing astonishing about such simple math, in order to decode the matrix of the Messianic clock to consummation. This is the matrix revealed in this book—the dates of creation and doomsday, as concealed in Daniel's prophecy.

What is evident is that in past millennia, mankind lost the data when time began. It became concealed for the wise (Maskilim) to decode the last days. Jesus said there is nothing hidden that shall not be revealed. He said, "When you see the Abomination of Desolation stand at the Holy Place let the reader understand." [63]

Jesus foretells that it is then that the calendrical distortion will be corrected and the enigma deciphered, just before the end of time. The timeline given, which Daniel was to seal and conceal, would be revealed in the last days by divine order. Jesus gave us the master key, when he said:

> "So when you see standing in the holy place 'the abomination that causes desolation,' spoken of through the prophet Daniel—let the reader understand." [64]

In attempting to decode the sealed Messianic Clock, we must clear the optical issue of calendars. It must be noted that the first dilemma we face is caused by the confusion of the world calendars, all being different and contradictory. Some were factual or regal calendars, based upon accession of rulers.

The lack of a single universal calendar made it impossible to calculate the proper time from creation. To add to the confusion, some calendars were based on the Lunar year, some on the Solar year, some on the Luna-Solar year, and some on the Sirius year. All major Kingdoms had their own methods to calculate time.

The Daniel timeline is the only authentic calendar to doomsday, given to him by the angel Gabriel. Jesus said it would be deciphered when you see the Abomination of Desolation standing at the Holy Place.

In order to fully appreciate the problem, we need to find out the source of the most ancient calendars. There is no doubt that the major ancient world calendrical systems are of Sumerian origin. These have been distorted by adaptations to different cultures and kingdoms, such as the Egyptian, Babylonian, Greco-Roman, Chinese and Mayan, as well as the Chronicle of the Jubilees found in the book of Enoch. Our Julian calendar is the best attempt to establish a universal timeline. Julian tried to correlate and synchronize world calendars and events to create the modern western calendar.

The ambiguous and distorted data inherently flawed our present day calendar. The Book of Jubilee timeline, the Daniel concealed timeline and Julian calendar converges and aligns on the date of Jesus baptism. This establishes the fact that Jesus was born 30 years before the end of 4,000 years from creation. He was born under the law; He was baptized to fulfill the law.

The baptism of Jesus marked the beginning of the dispensation of grace. The Julian calendar calculates from Jesus' birth whereas Biblical calendar counts from Jesus baptism when the dispensation of the law ended. Exactly 2,000 years preset for each dispensation. Therefore the Julian calendar is 26 years off the Biblical dispensational calendar.

The year 26 A.D. equals what we would call the year zero in Biblical chronology for the Dispensation of Grace. Jesus began His ministry in the 81st Jubilee exactly 4,000 years from creation. The Julian Western Calendar is accurate regarding Jesus' baptism and end of the

Dispensation of the Law. God calculates from this point for the Dispensation of Grace.

The baptism of Jesus defines time past, present and future. It establishes Rosh Hashanah, 4026 B.C., as the beginning of time. This event reveals the creation date concealed through the ages. We could not know exactly when the end will come until we corrected the calendric distortion using Biblical milestone of Jesus baptism and the sign of the Abomination of Desolation spoken by the prophet Daniel. The Abomination of Desolation confirms the same date for creation. These issues constitute the main focus of this book on Biblical chronology.

The Bible gives us empirical truth—infallible, inerrant and eternal. The truth of God's Word is proven and tested over the millennia. Jesus promises that the wise will understand the time of the end of the world which was sealed and concealed by the prophet Daniel, when they see the erection of the Abomination of Desolation. This event would declassify the sealed information and reveal to His chosen people the date preset for the end of the world. God promised: "He that reads will understand." [65]

Revelation and not rationality will reveal these things to the wise, as they follow the clue given by Jesus. God will unseal those secrets to His servants, when they follow the lead He gave them. The compromised, carnal church will not receive this divine revelation, because the spirit of delusion controls their deceived minds to adhere to false assumptions of gap theory, sanctioned by the religious establishment.

THE ORIGIN OF THE JEWISH CALENDAR IS NOT BIBLICAL

The Jewish calendar is not holy, for it is not from the Holy Bible. The Jewish people were chosen to be the custodian of the timeline from God, passed on to them by the patriarchs and nabi (prophets) of old. Tragically, they went astray when they adopted the Babylonian calendar during the Babylonian captivity. This concealed the timeline. It distorted the original Biblical calendar. It sealed the revelation until the Abomination of Desolation was erected at the Holy Place, spoken of by the prophet Daniel.

The present Jewish calendar was adopted from the Babylonian complex calendar of Nippur. It was based upon an ancient planetarium aligned to the Zodiacal constellations and the twelve Olympians of the Sumerian Pantheon. Each constellation had a celestial counterpart among the twelve members of the solar system, and each was honored for one month in the annual cycle of a twelve-month year. The Sumerian term for month is Ezen, meaning festival, because each month was devoted to celebrating the worship of one of the 12 supreme gods.

Back in time, ancient Babylonian history credited the Anunnaki (fallen angels or the sons of God) who took female earthlings as wives, with developing the calendar of Nippur. The book of Genesis and other Bible passages record these marriages as true facts. The Biblical name for these beings is "Nephilim."

> "And it came to pass, when men began to multiply on the face of the earth, and daughters were born unto them, that the sons of God saw the daughters of men, that they were fair, and they took them wives of all which they chose." [66]

It is important to note the word Nephilim literally means *those who have come down, who descended from heaven to earth.* The word is usually translated in our Bibles as *giants.* In Hebrew, the word is Anakim, which is actually a rendering of the Sumerian word Anunnaki. The Anakim were sons of Elohim, the God of heaven, who were cast down from heaven (fallen angels). They descended down and took earthlings, daughters of Adam, as wives.

The bible says about their offspring, "They bear children to them, the same became mighty men, who were of old, men of renown." [67] They established ancient royal bloodlines that ruled the earth. They originated the Babylonian calendar.

THE HISTORICAL PARALLELISM BETWEEN
BABYLONIAN AND HEBREW CALENDARS

The Sumerian and Akkadian texts credit the Sumerian Anunnaki for developing the calendar of Nippur. Its chronology began in 3761 B.C. It was developed to deceive mankind into worshipping the twelve Olympians of the Sumerian Pantheon. During the post-Babylonian exile, the Jewish people adopted this calendar and continue to use it to this day. To attest to this fact, here are the Babylonian-Jewish parallels and name adaptations for the 12 months in each culture:

Babylonian	Jewish Adaptations
1. NISANU	NISAN
2. AIARU	IYYAR
3. SIMANU	SIVAN
4. DUZU	TAMMUZ
5. ABU	AB
6. ULULU	ELUL
7. TASHRITU	TISHRI
8. ARAHSAMNU	MARHESHUAN
9. KISIMU	KESLEV
10. TEBETU	TEBET
11. SHABATU	SHEVAT
12. ADDARU	ADAR

Great caution must be advised in the use of this calendar for Biblical chronology. The Nephilim developed the Babylonian calendar adopted by the Jews, which unfortunately is referred to by most Biblical scholars for Biblical chronology and predictions of the end of time to disillusion the people of God. The Bible tells us that the devil is the father of lies and his calendar cannot be trusted.

This calendar is based upon his agenda to deceive the people of God. The Jewish calendar is not based upon revelation, but was originated by Satan's desire to mislead God's people.

As you may recall, when the angel Gabriel was sent to Daniel to give him the accurate timeline, the devil detained Gabriel for three weeks, to stop him from delivering to Daniel the accurate timeline to doomsday. This should tell you how much Satan hates mankind having the Messianic clock. The archangel Michael had to come to rescue Gabriel.

The devil tried to prevent you and me from receiving this vital information, critical for our future in these last days. He is still fighting to keep you ignorant regarding this most critical revelation. He doesn't want you to find out the Truth, because it is vital information for your survival in these last days.

> "But the prince of the kingdom of Persia withstood me one and twenty days: but, lo, Michael, one of the chief princes, came to help me; and I remained there with the kings of Persia. Now I am come to make thee understand what shall befall thy people in the latter days: for yet the vision is for many days." [68]

Scriptures make it clear that the devil is the prince of Persia, who in fact developed the calendar of Nippur to deceive mankind, and to keep them ignorant of when the end will come.

The devil never fought an angel delivering a message to mankind. He didn't fight Gabriel when He was sent to tell Mary regarding the first advent of the Messiah, yet He fought Gabriel, trying to prevent him from revealing the accurate timeline to the end, because this is the most critical information on Planet Earth.

Tragically, the post-exile rabbis adopted the date of creation from the Babylonian calendar and chronology. In the 10th century, in the "Standard Guide to Jewish and Civil Calendars," by Fred Reiss, they made the date official to this day. One should also note that it took hundreds of years before Jewish people adopted this date of creation.

Once you know the last days, it is easy to backtrack and calculate the first day. Praise God that Michael triumphed over Satan and released Gabriel to come down and give Daniel the correct calendar.

Daniel wrote the timetable to doomsday and sealed the information until the last days, for the wise to decipher in order to instruct many. Jesus gave us the key to unlock the seal when He said, "when you see the Abomination of Desolation, let him that reads Daniel understand." [69] Obviously if the devil was so opposed to mankind receiving this information, it is apparent why Gabriel told Daniel that the message would be concealed until shortly before the last days.

The Messianic Clock is anchored on a firm foundation of infallible and inerrant revelation given to Daniel. Daniel was given an exact and explicit timetable to doomsday. It was clear and unambiguous, so that, for the saints, the "day will not come as a thief in the night," [70] as the apostle Paul said. The people of God are illuminated and instructed by scriptures about the future. There are no surprises coming for the people of God as the Messianic Clock is revealed.

> "We have also a more sure word of prophecy, whereunto ye do well that ye take heed, as unto a light that shines in a dark place, until the day dawn, and the day star arises in your hearts. Knowing this first that no prophecy of the scripture is of any private interpretation. For the prophecy came not in old time by the will of man; but holy men of God spoke as they were moved by the Holy Spirit." [71]

Daniel's prophecy gives us the detailed account of the future. It gives us an accurate chronology of past and future events and signs to watch for. There is an amazing and perfect alignment today of Daniel's timeline and the world events foretold to happen before the end of the world. These perfect convergences of the prerecorded events in the world are signaling the end of days, since the sign spoken by Jesus (The Abomination of Desolation) already stands in the Holy Place on Temple Mount, as we will see in upcoming pages of this book.

Before our very eyes, we are seeing amazing last day events, which will soon dramatically affect you and your loved ones, before the glorious return of our Lord and Savior. The signs of the time confirm the Daniel's Messianic Clock to doomsday.

First we will need to examine the signs of the time and then the Daniel timeline, to see how both converge in our time. The events by themselves cannot be a reason to say these are the last days, as each generation has gone through perilous times, and subsequently made false assumptions that theirs was the terminal generation.

There must be a perfect correlation between the signs of the time and the Daniel timeline. The Messianic Clock given to Daniel and today's events are synchronizing in perfect precision, as we will see.

THE HANDWRITING ON THE WALL

The whole world can see the handwriting on the wall and the coming death of civilization, yet they can't interpret the writing. They don't know what it means to their future.

There is a universal panic and uncertainty. Leaders of the world are troubled, as they cannot see the solution to this global financial meltdown, nor to the catastrophic effects of climate change. The situation is exacerbated by the current energy crisis. Increasingly, debates over natural resources and other key issues have become nothing more than shouting matches and politicized confrontations.

Even more interesting is the fact that for the first time, the previously concealed prophetic Biblical chronology given by Gabriel to Daniel reveals the alignment of the Russian's and the Shiites in the last days. The Middle East political affiliations line up perfectly with the prophetic timeline.

God has provided classified information for the wise to discern the enigma of the coming terminal crisis. We are watching the literal fulfillment of Biblical prophecy unfold in the Middle East. The Babylonians could not read the writing on the wall, and today the world cannot read God's handwriting on Wall Street and Main Street. The handwriting is announcing the end of western civilization and the rise of the New World Order.

Today's headlines consistently confirm the signs of the time on the Messianic Clock. This perfect synchronization of the timeline and the events predicted by the prophets of old make it clear that we are living in the last days.

In the past, prophecy students tried to interpret prophecy in the light of world events, to no avail. Prophecy interprets world events. Global events do not interpret prophecy. This is critical: God's Word does not fit into world events, rather world events fit into God's plan for the ages. History does not interpret prophecy—prophecy interprets history. Prophecy predicts the future world events. Scripture defines the meaning of history.

It has been rightly observed that the Messianic Clock is inherently inerrant, and it establishes the historical and future time framework. Its timetable and prerecorded news headlines resonate throughout the ages, yet it remains a paradox, to be understood only by the wise, through revelation from God.

The Messianic Clock constitutes the only accurate timeline. Those who refute it are in an increasingly precarious position in these last days, as zero hour is upon us.

The Bible has a monopoly on truth, qualitatively and quantitatively. History gives us empirical evidence that the Bible is infallible. The Bible envisions the end of the world in our generation. It gives us a complete, cogent, vivid, specific and accurate panorama of the future until doomsday.

We know the future events in great details. This generation has an appointment with destiny, according to the Messianic Clock.

The calendar of Nippur is over 200 years off the mark, which is not surprising, because its authors, the Anunnuki priesthood, were dedicated to the worship of the Deceiver. The calendar is based upon historical distortion and false conclusions about when the world will end. Its creation date is wrong. Its purpose was to deceive mankind to worship the devil, not the Holy One of Israel.

In contrast, the Bible is a precise masterpiece, giving us impeccable, incisive datelines and a seamless tapestry of the ages. It resolves the riddle of the ages with startlingly succinct and infallible truth. The predictions laid out in the Holy Scriptures, concerning our future as part of the terminal generation, are so clear that even a novice would understand. They are written for ordinary people to comprehend.

The reason God sent Gabriel was to unmask the devils distorted, counterfeit calendar, which was superimposed on God's timetable. Daniel was instructed to write the information and conceal it for the wise (Maskilim) in the end of days. Once the information is deciphered, "the wise will instruct many", [72] since they will be the only ones to know what is really going on in the world.

The devil is opposed to anyone knowing the preset doomsday, when the present order will come to an end, because it marks a crushing defeat upon his kingdom. He also hopes that his deceptions will lead to more people not learning the truth until it is too late.

What is especially great is that the messenger angel, Gabriel, showed Daniel in a vision the detailed panorama of the end of history. This is how He vividly describes the preview for us of this glorious event of the end of days:

> "Behold, one like the Son of Man came with the clouds, and come to the Ancient of Days, and they brought Him near before Him. And there was given Him dominion, and glory, and a kingdom, that all people, nations, and languages should serve Him: His dominion is an everlasting dominion, which shall not pass away." [73]

The King is coming. The signs of the time are signaling His imminent advent.

The time on the Messianic Clock to this momentous event is approaching in our lifetime, since the erection of the "Abomination of Desolation" is far behind us. The Bible tells us when, where, and how, but not the final day and hour.

The prophet Daniel was given the date of the end of the age, but was not given the day and the hour of the Rapture of the saints. God is going to cut short the timeline for the sake of the elect. It is going to be earlier than you expect, because Jesus said:

"If those days had not been cut short, no one would survive, but for the sake of the elect those days will be shortened." [74]

As we noted before, Noah was told the year when the flood would come, but not the day and hour. Moses was told Israel would be in the wilderness 40 years. He also was not given the day and hour that Israel would cross the Jordan into the Land of Promise. Jeremiah was told that Israel would be in exile in Babylon for 70 years, and again, he was not told the day and hour.

This establishes the Biblical precedent. This is the prophetic paradigm: God reveals the timeline, but never the day and hour. Noah knew when the end was coming. Moses knew when Israel would enter the Promised Land. Jeremiah knew how long until Israel would return from exile. God revealed to Daniel when this age would end, just not the day and hour.

CHAPTER FOUR

THE MESSIANIC CLOCK: ANCIENT JEWISH WEDDING PARADIGM

According to ancient Jewish tradition, when a son was engaged, he would go home and prepare for the bride. Only the father would know the day and hour, when he is satisfied that everything is prepared and ready. When asked, the son would tell everyone, "I don't know the day and hour that the father has set." The son knew the time, but not the exact day and hour, when the father would say, "Now." The bride had to be ready to go at a moment's notice.

The father kept the day and hour secret within the traditional time window. Everybody knew it could happen anytime. We know the time window. It is revealed in God's Word when the Father will say to His Son, "Go bring your bride."

In Jewish tradition, the father gave so many signs to indicate that everything was almost ready for the blessed occasion. The Word of God gives us all the signs to look for, to reveal when the time is near.

THE FEASTS OF THE LORD

The seven feasts of the Lord begin with Passover, which celebrates the deliverance of Israel from Egypt. These feasts are divine appoints. Most prophetic events took place during these feasts. Jesus was born at the Feast of Tabernacles, baptized at Rosh Hashanah, crucified at Passover, rose again on the Feast of First Fruits, and the Holy Spirit was poured upon the church on the Feast of Pentecost. Paul calls these feasts "shadows of things to come." [75] These feasts of the Lord are God's calendar, serving as shadows of things to come.

The Feast of Trumpets was known as the feast where no one knew the day or hour, because it was based upon the sighting of the new moon. They knew the window but not the day and hour.

After you see all the pieces of the puzzle provided in the scriptures, you will be able to see why the apostle Paul said, "Ye brethren are not in darkness, that that day should overtake you as a thief." [76]

During the expected window for the Feast of Trumpets, especially in the year of Jubilee, the whole nation looked to Temple Mount in anticipation to hear the sudden trumpet sound. In addition, the priests lit a fire on the mountaintop at the sighting of the new moon. This was a sign to the waiting people, who did not know the exact day or hour when the new moon would appear in the Eastern sky. That day did not overtake them as a thief—they anticipated it to come any day.

The feasts of the Lord were dress rehearsals of what was prophesied to happen in the future. The people of God would know the time window, but not the exact day or hour when the trumpet would sound.

THE FEAST OF THE LORD AS HISTORICAL DIVINE APPOINTMENTS

In Leviticus chapter twenty-three, the feasts of the Lord are also referred to as the appointments of the Lord. Historically. The seven feasts of the Lord are God's appointments with mankind. Through the ages, God has synchronized the cosmic signs with the Feasts of the Lord to signal a divine appointment and a change of season.

The Talmud says the blood red moon is a sign of coming war. In the last millennium, there have been three sets of blood red moons within the same Jewish year, during feasts of the Lord. In each event, it signaled paradigm changes and fulfillment of prophetic events.

1. The Spanish Inquisition
   a. Passover, April 2, 1493
   b. Sukkoth, September 25, 1493
   c. Passover, March 22, 1494
   d. Sukkoth, September 15, 1494
2. Israel War of Independence
   a. Passover, April 13, 1949
   b. Sukkoth, October 7, 1949

      c. Passover, April 2, 1950

      d. Sukkoth, September 26, 1950

3. Israel Six Day War

      a. Passover, April 24, 1967

      b. Sukkoth, October 18, 1967

      c. Passover, April 13, 1968

      d. Sukkoth, October 6, 1968

On the Messianic Clock, when the signs in the heavens align with the feast of the Lord, it is a divine appointment for mankind. These alignments signal that major events are going to happen that will change the course of history.

HISTORICAL SET TIME FOR JUDGMENT

The month of Aviv in the Hebrew calendar is called the dark time, a time of lamentation and mourning. It is historically a preset time of judgment on the Messianic Clock. The 9th of Aviv has often been the Day of Judgment. It is the day that the 10 spies brought back a bad report to Moses and the children of Israel. It resulted in the deaths of 3 million people, after they left Egypt and wandered for 40 years in the wilderness. At the end of those 40 years, the next generation of the children of Israel crossed over into the Promised Land.

To show that God is a date setter, here are some of the subsequent judgments that also occurred on the 9th of Aviv, hundreds or even thousands of years after the 10 spies' report.

1. 600 B.C. —Destruction of the First Temple by Nebuchadnezzar
2. 70 A.D.   —Destruction of the Second Temple
3. 1290 A.D. —Jews kicked out of England
4. 1492 A.D. —Jews kicked out of Spain
5. 1914 A.D. —World War I
6. 1940 A.D. —Hitler proclamation to kill the Jews
7. 2005 A.D. —The Gaza Evacuation

Throughout history, God has kept this date as an appointment for judgment of His people. The Messianic Clock is specific, and everything happens at the precise, preset time.

CHAPTER FIVE

MESSIANIC CLOCK: THE GENESIS TIME TEMPLATE

Foreshadowed in the creation's six-day duration is a prophetic timetable, a blueprint of the Messianic Clock of the ages. The six day creation order outlines a definitive timetable of the ages to the end of time, followed by mankind's 1,000 year Sabbath Rest, on the seventh day. The end of six days of mankind's labor on earth will usher in the millennium rest.

The model was laid at creation. The paradigm of the ages, laid out in the creation template, reveals God's master plan of the ages. This is a precise schedule, predetermined in eternity past and preset in creation. The Messianic Clock is embedded and concealed in the six days of creation.

Throughout history, God repeatedly and consistently foretells the end from the beginning. "I have declared the former things from the beginning; They went forth from My mouth, and I caused them to hear it. Suddenly I did *them,* and they came to pass." [77] The timetable to the end of days is established by the six days of creation. Subsequent events and prophecies further bear witness to God's precise timetable, embedded in the six days of creation, told in Genesis:

> "And God saw everything that he had made, and, behold, it was very good. And the evening and the morning were the sixth day." [78]
> "Thus the heavens and the earth were finished, and all the host of them. And on the seventh day God ended His work, which He had made; and He rested on the seventh day from all His work, which He had made. And God blessed the seventh day, and sanctified it: because that in it He had rested from all His work which God created and made." [79]

It is important to note the six days of creation were God's exact master plan for the ages. This truth is echoed throughout the centuries. Enoch is believed to have received the revelation from God that judgment will come for all mankind after 6,000 years. He was the first to preach about the end of the world and the coming judgment at the end of mankind's six days of labor.

> "And Enoch also, the seventh from Adam, prophesied of these, saying 'Behold, the Lord cometh with ten thousands of His saints, to execute judgment upon all, and to convict all that are ungodly among them of all their ungodly deeds which they have ungodly committed, and of all their hard speeches which ungodly sinners have spoken against Him." [80]

Hebrew tradition says God revealed to Enoch that there was a correlation between the six days of God's work and six days of man's work on earth. God established the precedent of a six-day workweek as a prototype of things to come for mankind.

The six days of creation constitute the basic timeline to the end of time, when man's work on earth will be over. This brings us back to the empirical truth that God tells of the end from the beginning. This is an essential characteristic nature of God. He has a master plan, a blueprint, upon which subsequent acts of God are built.

By far the most crucial insight in deciphering the Messianic clock is the revelation that the six days of creation are the foundational design of the ages. There are no coincidences in the divine plan, no after thoughts. He chronicled the future ages in the six days of creation with absolute precision. This is so fundamental, so ultimate a fact, that it established the divine timeline. All subsequent prophecies neatly fit into this predominant underlying timetable.

There is no question that our God is a God of order. The Bible explicitly sets forth the timeline from the dawn of time. The countdown began on the first day of creation to the end of the age.

As the architect of the universe and time, God made a perfect statistical correlation between the two. This parallel similarity is by divine design to reveal the end from the beginning. When we understand the original blueprint in creation, we can understand all the subsequent timelines revealed in the prophetic predictions of the prophets.

The divine master plan is revealed from the very beginning. God tells the end from the beginning. The beginning for humanity is the Genesis creation story.

In a real sense, the book of Genesis gives mankind the original time map to the end of days. We are time travelers to our heavenly abode. There is a much-defined timeline to our destination that God established from the genesis of time. God rested after six days, so in a similar fashion will man enter into his rest.

There is an end to man's work and suffering at a very specific and definite date encoded in Genesis. It is a divine pattern for God to tell the end from the beginning. The book of Genesis is a factual guide to the end. Therefore it is crucial to have proper understanding of the Genesis creation timeline template, in order to understand prophesies.

Solomon said, "There is a set time for every event under heaven, a season for everything." [81] God wants us to know the times and seasons He has set. God does not want us to grope in darkness with no clue about when the end shall come.

THE CREATION MATRIX

The precise, distinctive time framework instituted by God in the six days of creation established a time span of 6,000 years for the ages. It accurately lays out the time line from the beginning to the end. God designed time to fulfill His plan and purpose, according to the times and seasons He preset. He preordained and predetermined everything at creation.

There is no doubt the Bible reveals remarkable details of the ages, the sequence of events, and, in many cases, even the timing. In 1800 A.D., Bishop Thomas quotes Isaac Newton who observed the precision with which Biblical prophecy is fulfilled throughout the ages. He wrote, "History is the great interpreter of prophecy. Prophecy is, as I may say, history anticipated and contracted; history is prophecy accomplished and dilated, and the prophecies contain the fate of most considerable nations and the substance of the most memorable transactions in the world, from the earliest to the latest times."[5]

God preeminently said in the book of Isaiah, "I AM the First and I AM the last and beside Me there is no God . . . . I appoint the ancient people and the things that are coming and shall come." [82] In the creation order He appointed the things to come. He set the clock to run out at the end of 6,000 years. The countdown began at the moment of creation.

CREATION TO DOOMSDAY

Time began on Rosh Hashanah, Tishri I, 4026 B.C. The Messianic Clock began to tick to doomsday. Time as we know it began. It is particularly important to note that in six literal days, God restored the earth that was without form and void. From nothingness, He spoke and spanned and floated the galaxies, the sun, moon and planets, 100 billion stars in 100 galaxies 13 billion light years away (according to our limited present scientific knowledge of the vastness of the universe). The Bible simply says:

> "In the beginning God created the heaven and the earth.
> And the earth was without form, and void; and darkness
> was upon the face of the deep. And the spirit of God
> moved upon the face of the waters. And God said, 'Let
> there be light and there was light . . . . And God saw every
> thing that He had made, and behold, it was very good. And
> the evening and the morning were the sixth day." [83]

---

[5] Newton, Bishop Thomas, "On the Prophecies," p. 635 (1852 ed.)

Divine time is fundamentally cyclical. The point of origination is the point of termination. The Torah tells us that God tells the end from the beginning. Just as planets orbit around the sun, the sun also adheres to a very definitive path and time span to complete its journey. History is orbiting on a definitive, preordained path and timetable to complete a cycle. Time is on a 6,000-year orbit to complete its cycle to zero hour. To know the beginning is to know the end.

THE CHURCH FATHERS KNEW THE
PROPHETIC TIME MAP TO DOOMSDAY

The prophetic time map is like a subterranean gold vein that runs throughout the ages, pinpointing events on the panoramic landscape of the ages. This Messianic Clock has never failed. As the saints of every age dug deep into the profundity of divine revelation, they were able to know what time it was. In every case they were startled at divine precision timing. They could tell the events scheduled for their generation. They were always ahead of the enemy.

The early church escaped from Jerusalem to Petra unharmed, before the fall of Jerusalem in 70 A.D. because of prophetic understanding of their immediate future.

God concealed the time map in His Word, so that the wise would seek and find it. All the clues and pieces of the puzzle are in the Bible, beginning in the order of the Creation events. God could have created the universe in the twinkling of an eye. He didn't need six days. He didn't take a night's sleep for rest. He simply did it to establish the time span for Adam's seed to discern the time allocated to us in this bubble of space, time and matter. Our time spectrum is limited to six days of labor, until we enter our eternal rest in Paradise.

6,000 YEARS PRESET TIME FROM CREATION TO DOOMSDAY

Historically, the early church knew the timetable to doomsday. The church father Lactantius, in the Divine Institutes in the fourth century, wrote that Jesus would return at the end of 6,000 years from creation, and the last 7 years would be a time of great tribulation.[6]

IRENAEUS IN A.D. 150 'AGAINST HERESIES'

"This is an account of the things formerly created, as also it is a prophecy of what is to come. For the day of the Lord is a thousand and in six days created things were completed: it is evident, therefore that they will come to an end at the sixth thousand year."

LACTANTIUS, IN THE DIVINE INSTITUTES SAYS:

"But we, whom the Holy Scriptures instruct, do know of the truth, know the beginning and the end of the world, respecting which we will now speak in the end of our work. . . . Therefore let the philosophers who innumerate thousands of ages from beginning of the world know that the "six thousandth" year is not yet completed, and that when this number is completed, the consummation must take place."

THE EPISTLE OF BARNABAS:

"And God made in six days the works of His hands; and He finished them on the seventh day, and He rested on the seventh day and sanctified it. Consider, my children, what that signified: 'He finished them in six days.' The meaning of it is thus: in six thousand years, the Lord God will bring all things to an end.

Therefore, children, in six days, that is in six thousand years, shall all things be accomplished. And what is it that He saith 'and rested the seventh day'? He meaneth this: that then His Son shall come and abolish the season of the wicked one (the Antichrist) and judge the ungodly, and

---

[6] Lucius Caelius Firmianus Lactantius, "The Divine Institutions," (Divinarum Institutonum Libri VIII

shall change the sun and the moon and stars, and then He shall gloriously rest in the seventh day."

The epistle of Barnabas confirms this: that Antichrist will rise before the Lord comes back at the end of time. The next major event in our day is the rise of Antichrist.

The Epistle of Barnabas says:

> "for with God one day is a thousand years, as God Himself testifies saying, 'Behold a day for man shall be 1,000 years.' Therefore children, in six days, that is 6,000 years, shall all things be accomplished." [7]

The Apostle Peter, in the Holy Scriptures, declares:

> "But the heavens and the earth, which are now, by the same word, kept in store, reserved unto fire against the Day of Judgment and perdition of ungodly men. But, beloved, be not ignorant of this one thing, that one day is with the Lord *as a thousand years, and a thousand years as one day.*" [84]

Undeniably, the Word of God tells us exactly, precisely, definitively, concretely and irrevocably that 1,000 years is equivalent to one day. This is infallible and unchangeable. Therefore God gave man 6,000 years before the end comes. God encoded this timetable in Genesis in the Old Testament, and He decoded the riddle in the New Testament. It was enfolded in the last 4,000 years, and unfolded 2,000 years ago.

God has given us a clear timetable until the end of history. He expects us to dig deep into the scriptures to find the Messianic clock. We are to

---

[7] Reference is Epistle of Barnabas, Chapter 15, Veiset

follow the Word like a vein of gold, digging deeper and deeper into great depth to discover His master plan of the ages.

The writer of the book of Matthew says, "Nothing is covered that shall not be revealed." [85]

Most notably in the past, God established the blueprint for the ages in types and shadows. There is not future Biblical prophetic fulfillment without a precedent. All prophecy is fulfilled according to historical precedent. The past reveals the future.

Job prayed for understanding of the double meaning of God's Word: the double fulfillment. He petitions God: "But oh, that God would speak and show the secrets of wisdom that they are double to that which is." [86]

It should also be noted that Solomon further confirms the duality of God's words in history, when he wrote, "I know that whatever God does, it shall be forever. Nothing can be added to it, and nothing taken from it. God does it, that men should fear before Him. That which is has already been, and what is to be has already been; And God requires an account of what is past." [87]

Understanding the ways of God is only possible through divine discernment that comes through prayer. Daniel prayed to God for enlightenment, illumination and instruction concerning the mystery of the end time. He asked God and He answered him:

> "And he said, 'Behold, I will make thee know what shall be in the last end of the indignation: for at the time appointed, the end shall be." [88]

It is particularly important to realize that the angel Gabriel was sent to clarify the Messianic Clock and the sequence of events leading to the end of the age.

Daniel was given full and complete understanding of the dateline. God does not want us to be ignorant about the End of Days. He wants us to know when the end will be. That is why He answered Daniel's prayer. He wrote the timetable that was given to him by Gabriel and sealed it for the wise to open in the last days. Fulfilled prophecies in the past give us the assurance that all future prophecies will be fulfilled as predicted.

Historically, the first Christian writer who attempted to calculate the age of the world from Holy Scriptures was Theophilus of Antioch. Concerning the whole account, he stated, "All times and years are made known to those who are willing to obey the truth." [8]

Basel the Great's "Hexaemeron" acclaimed that we can determine the first day of creation. He wrote, "You may indeed learn the very time when the foundation of the world was laid. If you return from this present time to former ages, you may endeavor studiously to determine the day of world's origin. Hence you will find when time began." [9]

Lactantius Firmianus made this bold assertion:

> "We who are trained by the Holy Scriptures in the know-
> ledge of truth, do know both the beginning and the end of
> the world." [10]

At the appointed time, this universe is designed to self-destruct at the word of His command. It's designed to last 7,000 years. It has a definite beginning and a definite end. It is wired to explode and burn into nothingness. God has established a timeline to dissolve our universe and create a new heaven and earth, after 7,000 years. The Holy Scriptures tell us:

> "Seeing then that all these things shall be dissolved, what
> manner of persons ought ye to be in all holy conversation
> and godliness, looking for and hasting unto the coming of
> the day for God, wherein the heavens being on fire shall

---

[8] Theophilus AD Autolycum 1.3.C
[9] Homily 1.c.6.8.55
[10] Lactantius, Divine Institutions 1.7.c 14. 7:211

be dissolved, and the elements shall melt with fervent heat?" [89]

HISTORICAL DATES FOR THE CREATION

Through the centuries, a great number of saints labored diligently in an attempt to formulate a complete chronology from creation to doomsday. The fact that they all disagree with each other demonstrates that the problems are profound. Here were some of the difficulties included, among others:

1. The uncertainty of accurate copying and transmission of original numbers recorded, since the Masoretic, Septuagint and Samaritan texts all disagree in this respect.
2. The possibility of missing generations in the genealogies, where nothing of Biblical significance happened.
3. The distortion and contradiction of ancient extra-Biblical calendars.
4. The difference of the length of the year.

One thing that all Biblical chronology assumes is a shorter chronology compared with the modern dogma of evolution. It should be recognized that the conclusions of most of the Biblical chronology scholars were based upon insufficient data, which led to speculative calculations with unproven and assumptions that cannot be tested. Here are some of the dates computed over the centuries for the origin of creation:

Bishop Ussher	4004 B.C.
Jewish calendar	3760 B.C.
Septuagint	5270 B.C.
Josephus	5555 B.C.
Kepler	3973 B.C.
Melanchthon	3964 B.C.

Luther	3961 B.C.
Light Foot	3960 B.C.
Hales	5420 B.C.
Playfair	4008 B.C.
Lipman	3916 B.C.

The creation date given in this book is not derived from extra-Biblical data, though it correlates with earth's early known history texts. It is based solely upon Daniel's timeline, given to him by Gabriel. It is Biblical. It stands on "it is written." God's Word is accurate. The Bible answers all the complex problems.

This conviction that the date is accurate is not simply based upon faith, but upon verifiable supportive evidence from history. A thorough understanding of Daniel's sealed and concealed message, regarding the dateline to doomsday, is necessary, if one is to understand the rest of prophecy.

The sealed message gives critical data that synchronizes the signs of the time and the Biblical timeline from creation to doomsday. It reveals the creation date and doomsday. The culmination of 6,000 years is the same termination point of the Daniel timeline.

THE MESSIANIC CLOCK: DOOMSDAY PRESET FROM CREATION

The Bible tells us that each "day" is 1,000 years. God set the paradigm, or the blueprint, of the span of time in the creation story given to mankind for work. God worked for 6 days to set the Messianic clock and to reveal that man will work for 6,000 years before he enters his rest in the millennium kingdom.

The creation days were a prototype of our work on earth. At the beginning of the seventh day, or the 7th millennium, Paradise will be restored. The Messiah will rule the planet for a literal 1,000 years and mankind will rest from the present suffering. This glorious event is finally going to take place in our generation.

The earth is like a plane flying through space to its destination at the end of 6,000 years. Presently, as predicted in prophecy, it is entering the stormy, interstellar turbulence and intergalactic upheaval. The powers of the heavens are being shaken. Jesus said there would be signs in the heavens to tell us we are almost home.

> "And there shall be signs in the sun, and in the moon, and in the stars; and upon the earth distress of nations, with perplexity; the sea and the waves roaring;" [90]

As we come close to the end of 6,000 years, science is predicting that in the next few years we are going to see major sunspots, possibly a reversal of magnetic poles, an increase in the moon's gravitational pull, killer protons and planetary tidal waves.

Bible prophecy calls these the signals of the approaching end of time. As we come to the final days of the 6th millennium, man's labor is almost over.

Time is running out. There are only fourteen years before we complete 6,000 years. We have entered the twilight zone. Every day counts for each person alive on earth today. These are days of visitation, and days of testing lie ahead of us. This is a time to prepare "as it was in the days of Noah." The extra-Biblical literature tells us that Noah built the ark in the last 5 years, before the 120th year, as God had told him. The rest of the people continued to mock him and his family as they prepared to escape.

Jesus, speaking about the last generation at the end of 6,000 years, said:

> "For then shall be great tribulation, such as was not seen since the beginning of the world to this time, no nor ever shall be." [91]

The ultimate future of this generation is seeing God restore the earth to its former glory. Ours is the most blessed generation. The time trajectory that began Rosh Hashanah, Tishri I, 4026 B.C., in the Garden of Eden, will finally be completed 6,000 years later. For 1,000 years, mankind will live in Paradise, before this old planet vanishes into eternal oblivion.

Our planetary system is a time bomb soon to blow up in a Genesis fireball, in an infinitesimal fraction of a second, at God's order, at the end of the millennium reign of Christ. God will create a new heaven and a new earth. The consummation of all things is at hand.

All history is mirrored in the Genesis story. The creation time structure of six days is a microcosm of the 6,000 years of human history. God is a God of order. God created man in His own likeness on the sixth day and He will transform mankind into His likeness and walk again with man in paradise restored in the six thousandth year.

As noted earlier, the Genesis chronological framework overlaps with other prophetic timelines into a consistent and precise (terminus) end. There is an amazing precision. This perfect synchronization is indicative of the Hand of God in human history. He is the Lord of history, both Author and Finisher. History bears witness to the faithfulness of God's Word. God's timeline is infallible. This is an indisputable truth!

Biblical forecasts envision the facts, as they will happen in the future. These predictions must be taken literally word for word. They will come to pass. The divine timetable predetermines what happens in history.

The divine timetable or blueprint for this planet was established in the book of Genesis. On the first day, Rosh Hashanah, Tishri I, 4026 B.C., there began a precise, accurate, solid, and final schedule. It is written into the very fabric of the universe. The present creation is wired to explode into a super nova at the Kairos hour at the end of the seventh day. God set the timeline from the beginning.

Seven in the Gematria, is a number of divine perfection or completion. In 7,000 years, the plan of God for this present order of creation will be completed. He works everything according to eternal purposes, for His glory. This generation is the final generation on earth, before the transition. The 7th millennium is the Sabbath rest for the people of God, when Christ will rule as the Son of David. This will be a prelude to eternity. The kingdom of God will be established on earth for 1,000 years before He creates the new heaven and new earth (terra nova).

"And I saw a new heaven and a new earth: for the first heaven and the first earth were passed away; and there was no more sea . . . and He that sat upon the throne said, 'Behold I make all things new.' And He said unto me, write: for these words are true and faithful." [92]

Ultimately, this old earth will be vaporized, the sun will burn out, and the universe will once again become a desolate void. The whole cosmos will fade into oblivion. The stars will disappear into the blackness and emptiness of the vacuum of space. Suddenly, God will create a new heaven and a new earth.

It is clear that the Messianic Clock is embedded in the scriptures and is not a mere appendage; it is the main focus, the principal guide, because time is moving towards consummation, or *"sunteleia"* (wrap up). Time will soon transpire (end). The chronological map is pointing to the end of this age.

We are living on the borderline between this age and the age to come. How thrilling for those who are ready for the *"anastasis"* (resurrection of the dead) and the *"harpagesometha"* (the catching away) of the saints to meet the Lord in the air at the *"parousia"* (the appearing of the Lord).

The *"Ha Yom"* (the last day) is just approaching and the day of the redemption of His people. We are called to *"paratereo"* (to watch) as we are living in the last days. The people of God must now be full of *"apokaradokia"* (eager expectation). Our work on earth will soon be over. This is our blessed hope. The King is coming!

God has measured time. He established an amazing mathematical formula from the six days of creation to Daniel's Messianic clock; yet it all synchronizes into a perfect, precise dateline to consummation. There is a mathematical precision encoded in the Torah that only God could establish. It baffles human intelligence, yet it is straightforward and simple for the Maskilim (wise).

In a real sense it is an adventure for us to ride together in God's time machine, as we travel from the dawn of time (Rosh Hashanah, Tishri 1, 4026 B.C.) to the end of time, six thousand years later.

THE MESSIANIC CLOCK: GENISIS 7-DAY TIME TEMPLATE TO DOOMSDAY

Day	The Date	Years	The Event
0	Eternity Past *4026 B.C. Rosh Hashanah	0	Creation
1	4026-1000 years: 3026 B.C. Rosh Hashanah	1,000	Enoch Translated to Heaven
2	3026-1000 years: 2026 B.C. Rosh Hashanah	2,000	Destruction of Sodom and Gomorrah
3	2026-1000 years: 1026 B.C. Rosh Hashanah	3,000	The Glory of God Filled Solomon's Temple
4	1026-1000 years *26 A.D. Rosh Hashanah	4,000	Jesus baptized and God spoke from heaven
5	26+ 1000 years: 1026 A.D. Rosh Hashanah	5,000	Dispensation of grace / Holy Spirit on earth
6	1026 + 1000 years *2026 A.D. Rosh Hashanah	6,000	Completion of Six Days of Labor (6,000 years)
7	2026 + 1000 years 3026 A.D. Rosh Hashanah	7,000	The Millennium Rule of Christ The Sabbath Rest
8	3026 A.D. New Creation	Eternity Begins	New Heaven and New Earth

0* 4026 Rosh Hashanah, October 2, Creation
4* 26 AD Rosh Hashanah, October 2, Jesus Baptism
6* 2026 A.D. Rosh Hashanah, October 2, end of time

The Biblical Chronology B.C. is minus and A.D. is plus

CHAPTER SIX

ONE HUNDRED AND TWENTY JUBILEE YEARS
TIME TEMPLATE TO DOOMSDAY

There is a perfect correlation between the Genesis six-day Messianic clock timetable and the timeline given to Noah for the end of the world. When superimposed on this original timeline, it fits with impeccable precision.

"And the Lord said, 'My spirit shall not always strive with man, for that he also is flesh: yet his days shall be an hundred and twenty years." [93]

Suddenly, on Sunday, November 30, in 1,656 A.M. (Anno Mundi) years of the world from creation (according to the "Annals of the World" by Bishop Ussher), God commanded Noah to enter the Ark. The world was oblivious to the impending catastrophe.

"In the six hundredth year of Noah's life, in the second month, the seventeenth day of the month, on that day all the fountains of the great deep were broken up, and the windows of heaven were opened. And the rain was on the earth forty days and forty nights." [94]

As God promised, on Sunday, the 17th day of the second Jewish month Kisliv, on December 7, in the year 2349 B.C., God sent the rain on the earth for forty days and nights. The flood covered the earth for 150 days.

The water began to go down and after 17 days, on May 6, the Ark rested on Mount Ararat. The waters continued to abate and on the first day of the tenth Jewish month (Sunday, July 19), the tops of the mountains were seen.

After 40 days, on the 11th day of the eleventh month (Friday, August 28), Noah opened the window of the Ark and sent forth the raven. It never came back.

On the 18th day of the eleventh month (Friday, September 4), Noah sent out the dove, and she returned 7 days later, on the 25th day of the 11th month (Friday, September 11).

Noah waited another 7 days and sent the dove again. This time it returned at night with a leaf from the olive tree. He waited another 7 days, and on the second day of the twelfth month (Friday, September 18), he sent the dove out again, and it never returned.

On the first month of the Jewish year, on October 23, Rosh Hashanah, the surface of the earth was dry. Noah removed the cover of the Ark.

On the 27th day of the second month (on Thursday, December 18), God commanded Noah to leave the Ark. Noah sacrificed in thanksgiving to God for preserving his family. God made a covenant not to destroy this earth again by a flood. He gave Noah the sign of the rainbow as a confirmation and reminder to mankind of His covenant commitment.

NOAH'S FLOOD HISTORICAL FACT

The Genesis flood record is an accurate account of a genuine historical event. The record is reliable and proven by archeological evidence. There was a real Noah, a real Ark, and a real flood—real judgment sent by God as a blueprint of the coming end time judgment.

Noah's flood was recorded by other literary accounts outside the Bible.*

1. Sumerian, "Eridu Genesis" 1600 B.C. contains a record of a massive Mesopotamian flood, from which animals and people were saved in a large ship built by Ziusudra, King of Shurrupak.
2. Akkadian "Atrahasis Epic" 1600 B.C. contains a similar account of the flood story in the Eridu Genesis.
3. Assyrian "Epic Gilgamesh" 2000 B.C. contains a flood story.

The epic Gilgamesh is most detailed, and closest to the Genesis account.[11]

There are also geological evidences all over the world that prove the authenticity of Noah's flood, such as the existence of whale fossils buried hundreds of miles from the sea. These marine fossils have been found in the Sierras, the Swiss Alps, and the Himalayas. Frozen mammals have been found in Siberia, Alaska and Northern Europe. Many bones of extinct animal species have been found fissured in the rocks.

There is evidence of ancient cities found off the coasts of Cuba and Japan, and on the Mediterranean coast. [12]

Noah's flood was a blueprint of things to come. It set the precedent of the coming judgment of God.

> "But as the days of Noah *were*, so also will the coming of
> the Son of Man be." [95]

Noah was given a definitive, set time when the flood would destroy the earth. It was a paradigm of the future Messianic Clock.

> "And that he would shew thee the secrets of wisdom, that
> they are double to that which is! Know therefore that God
> exacteth of thee less than thine iniquity deserveth."

God establishes in the most clear and unambiguous way the timeline as to when His Spirit will cease from striving with mankind. God here gives again the Messianic Clock from creation to consummation.

The secrets of God's wisdom are "double to that which is." The Noahian timetable is double to that which is a precise timetable to the end of the ages. God superimposed the Genesis timeline in the Noahian

---

[11] P.Carleton, "Buried Empires, Earliest civilizations of Middle East," London Edward Arnold 1939

[12] Posner Source Michael, "The Globe and Mail," Montreal, Canada

timetable, since He was speaking of a time past the flood, to a dispensation in the distant future, when His Spirit will cease to strive with mankind. The preset time of the end of 120 Jubilee years correlates with and terminates at the end of the Daniel timeline.

God superimposed on the Genesis time template the Noahian time template to the end of days, when God's spirit will cease to strive with man, for over 4,500 years he has continued to reach out to man until today. Noah's generation was a prototype, a blueprint of things to come according to the words of Jesus:

> "But as the days of Noah were, so shall also the coming of the Son of Man be." [96]

The Spirit of God is still at work in our world. He has not ceased from striving with the children of man, because we are still in the dispensation of grace.

The fulfillment of this prediction is still in the future. The Spirit of God is still moving and drawing men to Himself because the time preset is not yet completed. He is still seeking and saving the lost. He desires that all men might be saved before it is too late. Since the days of Noah, there have been great efforts on the part of God's Spirit, striving and reaching out to the fallen human race to save them through the person of His Son, Jesus Christ.

The English word "strive" means, *to make great effort, to try very hard, with malice towards none, to contend, to compete, to struggle, to battle, to fight, to be in conflict, to oppose by contrariety of qualities.* God is doing all of the above today, to save this world from the coming judgment at the end of the preset time, when His Spirit will cease to contend for man's salvation after 120 Jubilee years.

God superimposed the Jubilee cycles to consummation upon Noah's timetable, clearly to warn future generations of the coming judgment, as it was in the days of Noah. God gave mankind 120 Jubilee year cycles from Creation to consummation. God only counts the Jubilee years: they are known as "the Year of the Lord."

"To proclaim the acceptable year of the LORD." [97]

The countdown of 120 Jubilee years began on Rosh Hashanah, Tishri 1, 4026 B.C. Noah was given a definitive, specific, concrete, precise timetable from creation to consummation when God's spirit would cease from striving with man. This timetable is inerrant and infallible. It synchronizes with the Genesis time template and Daniel's Messianic Clock. There is no other authentic timeline except the Biblical timeline, declared by the Creator.

The wickedness, mockery and judgment of Noah's generation were just a foreshadowing of the end of the age, and a warning for this terminal generation. The apostle Peter confirms that the same conditions of the wickedness and mockery will exist in this terminal generation, parallel to that of Noah's time. In his second epistle, Peter wrote:

> "Knowing this first, that there shall come in the last days scoffers, walking after their own lusts, and saying, where is the promise of His coming? For since the fathers fell asleep, all things continue as they were from the beginning of creation.
> For this they willingly are ignorant of, that by the word of God the heavens were of old, and the earth standing out of the water and in the water: whereby the world that then was, being overflowed with water, perished: but the heavens and the earth, which are now, by the same word are kept in store, reserved unto fire against the day of judgment and perdition of ungodly men. " [98]

We are living in the generation that Peter is talking about. We are witnessing perfect similarities between Noah's generation and ours. In the days of Noah, the earth was flooded at the end of 120 years. In our generation, God will judge the nations with fire at the end of 120 Jubilee years, from creation in 4026 B.C. There are less than 14 years before the end of the preset period.

Jesus, speaking about the timeline to the consummation, refers back to Noah, "as it was in the days of Noah so shall it be." [99] It was 120 years. God used Noah's timetable of 120 years as a blueprint of the end of time. Jesus confirms the Noah Messianic Clock timetable to the end of days. All Biblical prophecy has a precedent, as we have established, "they are a double to that which is." God established the Messianic Clock in Noah's calendar to the flood.

The 120 Jubilee years are statistically grouped into cycles or dispensations. The Messianic Clock is divided into three dispensations:

DISPENSATION OF CONSCIENCE
(4026 B.C. – 2026 B.C.)
The first 40 Jubilee years (40 x 50 = 2,000 years) from Adam to Abraham.

DISPENSATION OF THE LAW
(2026 B.C. – 26 A.D.)
The Second 40 Jubilee Years (40x50 = 2,000 years) from Abraham to Baptism of Jesus. Total from creation 4,000 years.

DISPENSATION OF GRACE
(26 A.D. – 2026 A.D.)
The Third 40 Jubilee Years (40 x 50 = 2,000 years) Jesus' Baptism to consummation. Total from creation 6,000 years.

CREATION DATE
80 Jubilee years recorded from Creation to Jesus Baptism in 26 A.D. Creation date according to Biblical Calendar 4000+26 = 4026 B.C.

This present epoch is the final cycle of God's redemptive work on behalf of mankind. The Spirit of God is striving with mankind to restore them to Himself before time runs out. We are living in the final days of the Dispensation of Grace, the final dispensation before consummation.

As we focus on the precision timetable encrypted in the sacred literature from antiquity, there is indisputable evidence that Biblical predictions are accurate and inerrant. The Biblical timetable to consummation is consistent, literal and definitive from the beginning. The chronology outline in the scriptures remains consistent and solid, throughout the ages.

God wants us to know and understand the Messianic Clock to consummation. God revealed it many times to many prophets without discrepancies. God's people today need to pray David's prayer in Psalm ninety, verse twelve, "So teach us to number our days, that we may apply our hearts unto wisdom." [100]

As we are fast approaching the end of the Dispensation of Grace and the final days, before the Spirit of God ceases to strive with mankind, we need to apply our hearts to wisdom. The five foolish virgins did not prepare for the midnight crisis. Jesus spoke of a man that built his house on the sand. It collapsed when the storm hit.

There is a storm coming and many people have their lives built upon the sand. As it was in the days of Noah, almost no one was ready, except Noah and his family. They believed the timetable and prepared for the coming crisis. Noah's generation was a prototype of this final generation. Jesus said the timeline would be shortened. Time is running out. It is time to run with God. You are living on borrowed time.

Biblical chronology is amazingly specific, accurate and clear, to the wise. The prophet Daniel was told to seal the prophecy until the last days, and that the wise in the end of days will decipher the enigma and instruct many. This is the purpose of this book: to warn you of the fact that time is running out. Get yourself prayed up and filled up.

Jesus said, "I have foretold you *all things*." [101] *All means all.* All the pieces of the puzzle have been supplied you. Precise timetables, specific end time events, vital information for your survival to escape from the momentous catastrophic events and the predetermined judgment of God impending upon this generation.

The cosmic conflict foretold of old is approaching. The storm of the ages is brewing on the eastern horizon. A whirlwind unparalleled in human history is about to engulf our world.

> "Behold, a whirlwind of the Lord is gone forth in fury, even a grievous whirlwind: it shall fall grievously upon the head of the wicked. The anger of the Lord shall not return, until He has executed, and till He has performed the thoughts of His heart: *in the latter days ye shall consider it perfectly.*" [102]

The wise will consider it perfectly. They will see it coming and run for cover. There is acceleration towards the consummation. The Bible gives us a clear picture of the approaching end time events. The matrix of the prophetic timetable is laid out in scripture, in types and shadows for us to see.

Biblical prophecy provides us an anchor of utmost importance, as we see the fulfillment of these ancient forecasts. The clouds are clearing and the panorama of the events leading to the consummation is becoming clearer. The words of King David are still true and becoming increasingly urgent. He said, "The secret of the Lord is with them that fear His name."[103]

God's exquisite, precision timetable, the Messianic clock, is rooted in the past predictions. History illustrates with clarity the embedded timeline concealed in types and shadows, as God does everything in duality, as discovered by Job in antiquity.

> "That He would show thee the secrets of wisdom that *they are double* to that which is." [104]

Noah's 120 years time template has a double meaning to that which is to come. Historical precedents of the divine precision of the Messianic

Clock timetable forecast by the prophets of God, gives us a clear picture of what time it is. Noah's 120 years, encoded the 120 Jubilee years, to when the Spirit of God will finally cease to strive with man. Jesus decoded the encrypted when he said, "as it was in the days of Noah so shall it be."[105]

The secret of God's timeline is double and precise in double fulfillment. The first fulfillment, time of Noah, as a type and shadow, a blueprint of the future fulfillment of the 120 Jubilee years when the spirit of God will cease to strive with mankind in the Hebrew year 5788, Julian year 2026 A.D. The plan of God is unalterable. The truth of God's Word safeguards us against speculative assumptions and irrationality concerning the future. The Messianic Clock is the only infallible source of truth written by men and inspired by God.

Biblical forecasts eradicate fear of the future and the gloomy visions of the doomsayers. The future envisaged by the Biblical prediction is the restoration of Paradise lost, and the ultimate liberation from deprivation and man's estrangement from God.

The idealized hope of the ages is union between God and man, heaven and earth. Biblical perception of the future, after 120 Jubilee years, is glorious beyond words. The eschatology of doom is focused on the transitional trauma that will last for a very, very short period of only 42 months.

The paranoia regarding the end of days delivers us from our present culture of hedonism and self-indulgence. The gods of materialism in our generation that have replaced worship of the true God, the Creator, will be wiped out in a few short years from now. The current geopolitical fragmentation of this present order of things paves the way for the Kingdom of God on earth, as promised from ancient times.

The end of the 120 Jubilee years is a reason for joyous anticipation of the glorious return of our Lord and Savior. The end of 120 Jubilee years (120 x 50 = 6,000) is equivalent to the 6,000 years (six days) predetermined by God for man's labor before the millennium rest. The calculations began on Rosh Hashanah 4026 B.C. and culminate on Rosh Hashanah 2026 A.D. The plan of God is amazingly precise. There are no contradictions or conflicting data. There is a marvelous precision to Biblical chronology.

The riddle of the Biblical Messianic Clock timetable has been sealed for ages until now, as predicted by the prophet Daniel, that the wise (Maskilim) in the end of days will decipher the encrypted dateline. The divine timeline is seamless, succinct and absolutely precise. Jesus gave the key to understanding the concealed timetable in the sacred literature in the Olivet discourse, when He said, "When you see the Abomination of Desolation standing at the Holy place, whoso reads will understand." [106] This date is confirmed in the Daniel Messianic Clock as we will see in the pages of this book.

Since the Abomination of Desolation now stands at the Holy Place, the seal has been broken for all to see and understand the mystery of the ages. The student of prophecy can no longer read this book and leave puzzled and scratching his head. The seal has been broken, the matrix of the divine timetable revealed.

This book is a clarion call for readers to prepare to meet your Creator. We are less than 14 years to the end of the 120 Jubilee years when the spirit of God will cease to strive with mankind. The end of time is Rosh Hashanah 5788, the Jewish Lunisolar reckoning.

This is the Biblical timeline that Jesus said "would be shortened for the sake of the elect". [107] Therefore, no man will know the day and the hour when the end will come within these last two seven year cycles left before doomsday.

A sudden end will come towards the end of the declared timeline of 120 Jubilee years, at the height of the global holocaust. The Antichrist will attempt to destroy all Jews and the armies of the world will gather outside Jerusalem for the Battle of Armageddon, but Jesus will intervene and rescue the Jews.

When we see the armies of the world surrounding Jerusalem, we will know that this is that, which was spoken by the prophets of old. It will be obvious, clear, visible and unmistakable to every saint. The wise (Maskilim) will look up, for they will know that their redemption draws nigh. It will be within that time when Jesus interrupts the Antichrist's agenda.

Jesus gave us all the signs to look for when He said, "When you see these things, look up, your redemption draws near." [108] Jesus gave His disciples another clue to look for in those last days: the astronomical signs (Thema Mundi) in the sun and the moon.

> "Immediately after the tribulation of those days shall the sun be darkened, and the moon shall not give her light, and the stars shall fall from heaven and the powers of the heavens shall be shaken. Then the sign of the Son of Man will appear in heaven, and then all the tribes of the earth will mourn, and they will see the Son of Man coming on the clouds of heaven with power and great glory. And He will send His angels with a great sound of a trumpet, and they will gather together His elect from the four winds, from one end of heaven to the other. " [109]

The Day of the Lord will not overtake them as a thief in the night, as the apostle Paul says. The saints on the earth will know the time of their visitation. They know the schedule. There will be a perfect alignment of world events and Biblical prophecy timeline.

Among the saints, there will be a universal collective expectancy of the imminent end, as they watch the signs of the times leading up to their glorious homecoming. There will be no uncertainty among the sons of God (b'nai Elohim).

All the scriptures indicate that the saints will be prepared and knowledgeable of the timing. Against this overwhelming Biblical evidence, it can only be explained that the fallacious assumption that no one will know when the end will come is both unscriptural and misleading to the people of God.

It is important to observe that all the scriptures speak with one voice: the saints will know the time of the second coming of Christ. The primary purpose of Biblical prophecy is to give the saints the timetable (Messianic Clock) and sequence of events leading to the end of days.

There is a growing prophetic expectancy in the world today of the imminent return of Jesus to this planet. Many people all over the world are contemplating the end of the world. They are trying to assess the signs of the times. While the organized church is busy trivializing, spiritualizing, etymologizing and allegorizing Biblical prophecy, real people in the real world are seeking to discern the signs of the times, as they feel something is in the air. They are watching economic meltdown, social upheaval, financial collapse and global confrontation between East and West, all while the organized church is at best asleep, and at worst in bed with New World Order.

People on Wall Street and Main Street alike know something big is about to happen in the global village. Everything is being shaken. Most don't know that what they are hearing are the footsteps of the coming Messiah. We have passed the point of no return

The world needs interpretation from God's Word regarding the meaning of all these events. We can ascertain from Biblical predictions the true meaning of events in our terminal generation. The future has a universal appeal. It is the most popular subject, because every living person is going there.

The Holy Scriptures give us a complete, cognitive, vivid picture with most startling details regarding our future. Unknown to most people, the deadline is revealed in the Messianic Clock timeline. It is a remarkable manifesto of the future. Mankind's grand adventure is about to terminate at the end of 120 Jubilee years, dating back from Rosh Hashanah, 4026 B.C., to Rosh Hashanah, October 2, 2026 A.D. when the Noahian time template expires.

Time on the Messianic Clock is incisive and definitive. We are living in the last days of the last days. For centuries mankind looked forward through the millennia to this generation and predicted the events of our day with astonishing details. Our generation has an appointment with destiny. The party is about to begin.

The royal invitation has been sent to everyone. All are invited. Don't miss the party—respond to Jesus' invitation.

"And Jesus answered and spoke to them again by parables and said: The kingdom of heaven is like a certain king who arranged a marriage for his son, and sent out his servants to call those who were invited to the wedding; and they were not willing to come. Again, he sent out other servants, saying, Tell those who are invited, See, I have prepared my dinner; my oxen and fatted cattle *are* killed, and all things *are* ready. Come to the wedding.
But they made light of it and went their ways, one to his own farm, another to his business. And the rest seized his servants, treated *them* spitefully, and killed *them.* But when the king heard *about it,* he was furious. And he sent out his armies, destroyed those murderers, and burned up their city.
Then he said to his servants, The wedding is ready, but those who were invited were not worthy. Therefore go into the highways, and as many as you find, invite to the wedding. So those servants went out into the highways and gathered together all whom they found, both bad and good. And the wedding *hall* was filled with guests. But when the king came in to see the guests, he saw a man there who did not have on a wedding garment.
So he said to him, Friend, how did you come in here without a wedding garment? And he was speechless. Then the king said to the servants, Bind him hand and foot, take him away, and cast *him* into outer darkness; there will be weeping and gnashing of teeth. For many are called, but few *are* chosen." [110]

The royal party is scheduled to begin before the preset time is accomplished in the Royal Palace of Heaven. The party will begin a little early and nobody knows the exact day or hour, because the days will be shortened for the sake of the elect. Jesus said He was returning to heaven to prepare a mansion for His bride, the Church. It has taken him 2,000 years to prepare for your homecoming.

> "Let not your heart be troubled: ye believe in God, believe also in me. In my Father's house are many mansions: if it were not so, I would have told you. I go to prepare a place for you. And if I go and prepare a place for you, I will come again, and receive you unto myself: that where I am, there ye may be also." [111]

The greatest tragedy is to be found not wearing a royal robe and consequently to be expelled from the City of God. Only born again children of God will enter the City of God, justified by faith alone, in Christ alone and born from above.

> "Jesus answered and said unto him, Verily, verily, I say unto thee, except a man be born again, he cannot see the kingdom of God. Nicodemus said unto him, How can a man be born when he is old? Can he enter the second time into his mother's womb, and be born? Jesus answered, 'Verily, verily, I say unto thee, except a man be born of water and of the Spirit, he cannot enter the Kingdom of God. That which is born of the flesh is flesh; and that which is born of the Spirit is spirit.
> Marvel not that I said unto thee, Ye must be born again. The wind blows where it wishes, and you hear the sound of it, but cannot tell where it comes from and where it goes; so is every one who is born of the Spirit.
> He who believes in the Son has everlasting life; and he who does not believe the Son shall not see life, but the wrath of God abides on him. " [112]

Religion will not give you access to the City of God; only a personal relationship with Jesus Christ will do that. You have to ask Jesus to come into your life, to forgive you and to become Lord and Savior of your life. He is the Way, the Truth and the Life. The man that went to the party without the royal robe represents those who are not born again, who will be cast out of the City of God. John, in the book of Revelation, saw who were cast out of the Holy City. This is what he wrote about their fate:

"And whosoever was not found written in the book of life was cast into the lake of fire." [113]

THE NOAHIAN MESSIANIC CLOCK:
120 JUBILEES* FROM CREATION TO DOOMSDAY

Date	Jubilee	Event	Scripture
4026 B.C.	0	Creation	Genesis 1:3
3026 B.C.	20	Enoch Translated to Heaven	Genesis 5: 22-24
2026 B.C.	40	Sodom and Gomorrah Destroyed	Genesis 19
1026 B.C.	60	The Glory of God Filled the Solomonic Temple	2 Chronicles 7: 1-3
26 A.D.	80	Jesus Baptized, God Spoke from Heaven	Matthew 3: 16-17
1026 A.D.	100	The Holy Roman Empire Claims to Replace the Jews, Organizes the Crusades	Revelation 3:9
2026 A.D.	120	The End of Time	2 Peter 3: 8-10

* A Jubilee is a 50 year cycle

CHAPTER SEVEN

THE DANIEL MESSIANIC CLOCK: BREAKING
THE SEAL OF THE ENIGMA OF THE AGES

"Now I am come to make thee understand what shall befall thy people in the latter days: for yet the vision is for many days." [114]

"But thou, O Daniel, shut up the words, and seal the book, even to the time of the end: many shall run to and fro, and knowledge shall be increased." [115]

Gabriel told Daniel exactly when the world would come to an end. He was given a precision timetable of the end time events and the predetermined consummation of the ages. He was told to seal the information until the time of the end, when the wise would decipher the encoded message and instruct many.

"And he said, 'Go thy way, Daniel: for the words are closed up and sealed till the time of the end. Many shall be purified, and made white, and tried; but the wicked shall do wickedly: and none of the wicked shall understand; but the wise shall understand." [116]

"And they that understand among the people shall instruct many: yet they shall fall by the sword, and by flame, by captivity, and by spoil, many days. Now when they shall fall, they shall be helped with a little help: but many shall cleave to them with flatteries. And some of them of understanding shall fall, to try them, and to purge, and to make them white, even to the time of the end: because it is yet for a time appointed." [117]

When Daniel began to seek God's plan for the ages, and the timetable of the advent of the Messiah, God sent Gabriel to reveal to Daniel the Messianic clock timeline, and the sequence of events leading to consummation of the ages, as we saw in the previous pages.

The devil fought against Gabriel and detained him for three weeks, to stop him from revealing to mankind the timetable to doomsday. Satan does not want anyone to know this vital information. Here is what Daniel says of his encounter with Gabriel:

> "Yea, while I was speaking in prayer, even the man Gabriel, whom I had seen in the vision at the beginning, being caused to fly swiftly, touched me about the time of the evening oblation. And he informed me, and talked with me, and said, 'O Daniel, I am now come forth to give thee skill and understanding. At the beginning of thy supplications the commandment came forth, and I am come to show thee; for thou art greatly beloved: therefore understand the matter, and consider the vision." [118]
>
> "And he said to me, "O Daniel, man greatly beloved, understand the words that I speak to you, and stand upright, for I have now been sent to you." While he was speaking this word to me, I stood trembling. Then he said to me, "Do not fear, Daniel, for from the first day that you set your heart to understand, and to humble yourself before your God, your words were heard; and I have come because of your words. But the prince of the kingdom of Persia withstood me twenty-one days; and behold, Michael, one of the chief princes, came to help me, for I had been left alone there with the kings of Persia. Now I have come to make you understand what will happen to your people in the latter days, for the vision *refers* to *many* days yet *to come*." [119]

The devil is doing everything to keep the people of God ignorant of what time it is. He is afraid they will get prayed up and filled up with God. The devil cannot defeat people who pray and are filled with God. Michael, the Archangel, had to fight to release this vital information to Daniel, for the terminal generation's use.

The devil is working overtime to keep you ignorant of the divine timetable to the end of the world. I cannot emphasize enough how Satan is planning a surprise attack on mankind in our generation. He will attempt to kill the wise (Maskilim) who will instruct many about the time, according to the Messianic clock. Satan will hunt to kill everyone who knows God's master plan.

Satan will try to put his insignia (666), the biochip implant, on the forehead or hand of every person, in these last days before the advent of the Messianic Kingdom.

Daniel asked Gabriel directly when the end will come:

> "And one said to the man clothed in linen, which was upon the waters of the river, 'How long shall it be to the end of these wonders?" [120]

He was given how long it shall be to the end of these wonders. God gave him a concise and precise Messianic clock timetable, both of the end of the world, and of the future events leading to the consummation of history.

When Gabriel told Daniel, "I am come forth to give you skill and understanding," he gave him the whole picture. All world events correlate with the chronology that was given to Daniel. This debunks all false teaching, which asserts that God does not want anyone to know when the end will come. Daniel was told everything about how much time is left before the end of the world. He was given the calendar of world events.

All through the centuries, God set dates for the four kingdoms that would rule the earth before the advent of the Messianic kingdom. These forecasts have never failed. The Biblical track record is perfect.

Historical evidence in the past six thousand years leads us to the simple conclusion that the timetables revealed in scripture are literal and straightforward. They never failed. The timeline is consistently accurate and infallible. The matrix of revelation is simple. The 66 books of the Bible do not give us a morass of differing views. This is why the saints today need to take God at His Word.

This is far more important today as we are fast approaching the deadline to history. It is sad that the end time eschatology is interpreted as fiction. What a tragedy! There is no fiction in the Word of God. All scriptures will be fulfilled literally, experientially, materially, physically and punctually. God said it—that settles it. It shall come to pass!

The wise will understand what time it is on the Messianic Clock, because God promised that in the last days, He would reveal the sealed message to the wise. Ask and it shall be given.

The seal has been broken and the chronogram code uncovered the mystery revealed and the predictions of the end unveiled. Jesus said when you see the Abomination of Desolation stand at the Holy Place the reader of Daniel's sealed prophecy will understand. Since the Abomination of Desolation stands at the Holy Place, the secrets have been revealed of both the events and timetable of ominous catastrophes preset to happen in our generation. It is no longer an enigma, it's now an open secret, the curtain has been pulled back and finally we can see into our immediate future.

CHAPTER EIGHT

THE MESSIANIC CLOCK: THE DANIEL ENIGMA UNVEILED
THE FOUR EMPIRES PREDICTED TO RULE BEFORE
THE ADVENT OF THE MILLENNIAL KINGDOM

The book of Daniel records King Nebuchadnezzar's prophetic dream that described the four empires that would rule the world before the Messianic Kingdom.

> "You, O king, were watching; and behold, a great image! This great image, whose splendor *was* excellent, stood before you; and its form *was* awesome. This image's head *was* of fine gold, its chest and arms of silver, its belly and thighs of bronze, its legs of iron, its feet partly of iron and partly of clay. You watched while a stone was cut out without hands, which struck the image on its feet of iron and clay, and broke them in pieces. Then the iron, the clay, the bronze, the silver, and the gold were crushed together, and became like chaff from the summer threshing floors; the wind carried them away so that no trace of them was found. And the stone that struck the image became a great mountain and filled the whole earth." [121]

The metallic image Nebuchadnezzar dreamt was suddenly destroyed. "You watched while a stone was cut out without hands, which struck the image on its feet of iron and clay, and broke them in pieces." [122] The whole enormous statue was broken and blown away by the wind. The Messianic Kingdom is the stone not cut with human hands.

The image was made up of various metals; the head was made out of gold, the chest and arms of silver, the belly and hips of brass, the legs of iron, and the feet and toes of iron and clay. Daniel gave the king the interpretation.

The image's head symbolizes Nebuchadnezzar himself, the Babylonian Empire. The silver chest and arms represent the second empire that followed the Babylonian Kingdom, Medo-Persia. The belly and hips of brass symbolize the Greek Empire.

The fourth Kingdom is the Roman Empire, represented by the two feet made of iron and clay. The ten toes represent the revived Roman Empire as the New World Order. They will rise in the last days and be composed of ten global economic regions. It will be a combination of (strong) iron nations and (weak) clay nations.

The ten toes [123] represent the New World Order, a one-world government headed by the Antichrist. This evil dictator will seek to obliterate mankind through nuclear holocaust, when cities will be turned into contaminated wastelands. The generation alive today will see these things. The Roman Empire has been revived and is orchestrating the rise of the New World Order, the final superstructure to rule the world and dominate the clay nations.

The ten toes are the global economic spheres of the New World Order, described in Nebuchadnezzar's "metallic" dream, as the final form of the last empire. It will rise on the earth before the Messianic Kingdom ("a stone was cut without hands" [124]) crushes and destroys the worldly kingdoms.

> "Whereas you saw the feet and toes, partly of potter's clay and partly of iron, the kingdom shall be divided; yet the strength of the iron shall be in it, just as you saw the iron mixed with ceramic clay. And *as* the toes of the feet *were* partly of iron and partly of clay, *so* the kingdom shall be partly strong and partly fragile.
>
> As you saw the iron mixed with ceramic clay, *they will mingle with the seed of men; but they will not adhere to one another,* just as iron does not mix with clay.
>
> And in the days of these kings, the God of heaven will set up a kingdom which shall never be destroyed; and the

kingdom shall not be left to other people; it shall break in pieces and consume all these kingdoms, and it shall stand forever.

Inasmuch as you saw that the stone was cut out of the mountain without hands, and that it broke in pieces, the iron, the bronze, the clay, the silver, and the gold—the great God has made known to the king what will come to pass after this. The dream is certain, and its interpretation is sure." [125]

Daniel predicted that the Messianic Kingdom would come during the time of the revived Roman Empire. History attests to the authenticity of his predictions. The fourth world empire has revived as the European Community by the Treaty of Rome in 1957, to set the stage for the New World Order.

Daniel describes our present terminal generation. All the predictions he foretold are unfolding before our very eyes. He gave us a precise timeline, specific details concerning the four empires that rose to rule the earth before the advent of the Messianic Kingdom—the stone cut without hands that will destroy the New World Order of the revived Roman Empire in the last days.

Daniel's prophetic texts are very definitive. We are able to decipher the mysteries of the ages. The predictions have been consistently accurate, and the Messianic Clock infallible throughout the ages.

The Daniel Messianic Clock points to this generation as the final generation. There is no doubt that what we have here in Daniel's interpretation of the metallic image in Nebuchadnezzar's dream is an accurate historical chronology to doomsday. It is straightforward history, written in advance.

The accuracy of these predictions is of crucial importance, as they identify the players on the stage in our generation. Everything is shaping up exactly according to Daniel's prophecy. On the heels of this text, it is imperative that we mobilize the saints for the last match and the last battle of the ages. History is rushing towards culmination in this current age.

We are watching the rise of the ten toes kingdom. Daniel tells us specific signs to look forward to in our generation. One world government, one world economy, and one world religion will each rise during these final days on earth. It will be a totalitarian government. It will implement global taxation on every financial transaction.

The taxes will be justified as the only way that a solution to climate change can be funded. A biochip implant with the number 666 and a personal identification number (P.I.N.) will be embedded under the skin on the hand or forehead. This chip will enable every person on earth to be tracked.

The New World Order will be a cashless society, and all transactions will be through electronic transfer, using the biochip implants. A person without the biochip will be unable to buy or sell.

> "He causes all, both small and great, rich and poor, free and slave, to receive a mark on their right hand or on their foreheads, and that no one may buy or sell except one who has the mark or the name of the beast, or the number of his name. Here is wisdom. Let him who has understanding calculate the number of the beast, for it is the number of a man: His number *is* 666." [126]

For the first time in history, the technology exists to track every person and every financial transaction on earth in real time. This brings a much greater immediacy to Daniel's prophecy, since events he predicted are happening now in our time, for the first time in history. As we cross-reference ancient prophesies with current events, it becomes quite evident that these are the last days.

The countdown to the apocalypse has begun on the Messianic Clock. The New World Order is emerging from two divisions of ancient Rome. The two legs of the Roman Empire represent the western empire and the eastern empire. The former Soviet Union represents the eastern division.

It will be revived as Eurasian Union of Gog and Magog as foretold by the prophet Ezekiel. [127] The western empire was based in Rome and the eastern empire in Constantinople. The eastern empire moved to Moscow. Both the western division and the eastern division have been revived. Today NATO represents the western interests and the eastern interests are spearheaded by Russia.

The final showdown between the western division and the eastern division will be played out in the battle of Armageddon. Israel will be ground zero for the confrontation. The "Land for Peace" conflict will be central to the coming Middle Eastern conflict between super powers. The western division will align with the Sunni moderate Arab Muslims, while Russia will align with the Shiite radical Muslims.

The Shiite nations led by Persia (Iran) will put an economic hook in Russia to support the Shiite rejectionists of the "Land for Peace" agreement, orchestrated by the western division of Rome—a NATO alliance with the Sunni moderate Arab nations.

"Now the word of the LORD came to me, saying, Son of man, set your face against Gog, of the land of Magog, the prince of Rosh, Meshech, and Tubal, and prophesy against him, 'Thus says the Lord GOD: "On that day it shall come to pass *that* thoughts will arise in your mind, and you will make an evil plan: You will say, I will go up against a land of unwalled villages;

I will go to a peaceful people, who dwell safely, all of them dwelling without walls, and having neither bars nor gates to take plunder and to take booty, to stretch out your hand against the waste places *that are again* inhabited, and against a people gathered from the nations, who have acquired livestock and goods, who dwell in the midst of the land. Sheba, Dedan, the merchants of Tarshish, and all their young lions will say to you, have you come to take plunder? Have you gathered your army to take booty, to carry away silver and gold, to take away livestock and goods, to take great plunder?" [128]

Sheba and Dedan represent the moderate Sunni Arab nations aligned with NATO. Tarshish represents NATO. This is the political alignment of the battle of Armageddon. The two legs of the revived fourth kingdom and their allies will gather together the entire world in the biggest battle of all time—the battle of Armageddon, over Israel.

The Antichrist will rise out of the fourth Roman Empire, revived and morphed into the New World Order. He will be Satan incarnate. He will rise from obscurity to global acclaim in a very short time.

Daniel tells us that the Antichrist will rise from the Roman Empire:

> "And in the latter time of the kingdom, when the transgressors have reached their fullness, a king shall arise, having fierce features, who understands sinister schemes. His power shall be mighty, but not by his own power; He shall destroy fearfully, and shall prosper and thrive; He shall destroy the mighty, and *also* the holy people." [129]

The Antichrist will bring false security and prosperity to the world, through his policy.

> "His power shall be mighty but not by his own power, and he shall destroy wonderfully and shall prosper and practice and shall destroy the mighty and the Holy people. And through his policy also he shall cause craft (economy) to prosper in His hand. And he shall magnify himself in his heart, and by peace shall destroy many. He shall also stand up against the Prince of princes, but he shall be broken without hands." [130]

His successes will cause him to magnify himself as god. His actions are documented and chronicled in advance. He will not be able to surprise the people of God.

The Bible furnishes us with a comprehensive, detailed picture of tomorrow's shockwaves, to prepare us for the last stand against the kingdom of darkness.

In Ephraim's book from the cave of treasures in the Dead Sea Scrolls, Ephraim wrote this about the time of the Antichrist:

> "At the end of the world and at the final consummation, suddenly the gates of the north shall be open. . . . They will destroy the earth and there will be none able to stand before them. After one week, seven years, that sore affliction (tribulation), they will be destroyed in the plain of Joppa. Then will the son of perdition appear of the seed of the tribe of Dan. He will go to Jerusalem and will sit upon a throne in the temple, saying, "I am Christ," and he will be borne aloft by legions of devils, like a king and law giver, naming himself god."

The world will be plunged into a series of horrific wars and nuclear holocaust. Finally the armies of the world will be gathered in the valley of Jezreel to fight the battle of Armageddon.

The Messianic clock places this cosmic battle at the end of the world. The accuracy of Daniel's interpretation of Nebuchadnezzar's dream is indisputable. It is accurate and infallible. The ultimate future he foretold is here—the consummation of all things.

The predictions concerning our days point to a grim picture of approaching cataclysmic upheaval and unparalleled calamity. These are the birth pangs of the coming Messianic kingdom. We live in the borderland between this age and the age to come. This generation will not pass away until all these things are accomplished.

Biblical prophecy has been your missing link to the future. The Messianic Clock encoded in the sacred scriptures reveals to you the shape of things to come—to keep you informed and ready. We are given explicit signs to look for during this period of transition. Antichrist's rise to power is the final chapter of the legacy of Satan's rebellion. He will not be a surprise to the saints, as the sacred scriptures give us the preset time of the end.

The Messianic Clock in scripture provides detailed descriptions of the dispositions of the forces, the terrain of the landscape, and the political alignments of Russia with the Shiite Muslims and NATO with the Sunni Muslims. The lineup is forming before our very eyes. Israel is in the eye of the storm.

The frontiersmen of the coming terminal confrontation are already on the scene. Jesus said that when you begin to see these things take place, raise your heads and look up, because your redemption is drawing near.

DANIEL'S DESCRIPTION OF THE WORLD EMPIRES
This Is How Daniel Interpreted The King's Vision

PERIOD	SYMBOL	EMPIRE	DANIEL'S PROPHETIC DESCRIPTION : DANIEL 2
600 B.C.	Head of Gold	Babylon	"Thou are this head of gold."
539 B.C.	Chest of Silver	Media-Persia	"After thee shall arise another kingdom inferior to thee."
334 B.C.	Belly and Hips of Brass	Greece	"Third kingdom of brass, which shall bear rule over all the earth."
63 B.C.	Legs of Iron	Rome	"The fourth kingdom shall be strong as iron: forasmuch as iron breaketh in pieces and subdueth all things . . . shall it break in pieces and bruise."
2012-2026 A.D.	Ten Toes of Iron and Clay	New World Order	"The kingdom shall be divided . . . . So the kingdom shall be partly strong, and partly broken."
2026 A.D.	The Stone Cut Without Hands	The Messianic Kingdom	"In the days of these kings shall the God of heaven set up a kingdom, which shall never be destroyed."

CHAPTER NINE

THE GABRIEL MESSIANIC CLOCK: THE SIGNS OF THE TIMES ARE ALIGNING FOR THE FIRST TIME IN HISTORY

We will synchronize signs of the time and the Messianic clock given to Daniel by Gabriel. This is the dateline from creation to the end of time. Daniel's prophecy reveals the mystery of time. It gives the blueprint in which all time is defined. Jesus tells us that the concealed mystery would be unveiled by one single event that will take place on Temple Mount at the Holy Place.

This single prophetic enigma would unveil the timeline to the end of days as predicted by Daniel. It is the master key to decoding the sealed message. It is the code breaker to the Daniel time enigma.

> "When ye therefore shall see the abomination of desolation, spoken of by Daniel the prophet, stand in the holy place, (whoso readeth, let him understand.) [131]

Jesus said, "Whoso readeth, let him understand." This tells us the Daniel timeline will be unsealed and made understandable when the Abomination of Desolation is revealed. The true timeline to doomsday will be decoded.

The Biblical six days of man's labor before he enters the Sabbath rest in the seventh millennium will all be made clear, according to God's ancient Messianic Clock when we see the Abomination of Desolation. This is the crux of the matter: the Abomination of Desolation is the code breaker of end time prophecy. It is important to realize that only this single event is the decoder of the mystery hidden through out the ages. There is no other key to breaking the seal. Jesus holds the key—He is the Alpha and Omega. He revealed the code breaker to the disciples. Based upon this revelation, the mystery has been unveiled, as we are about to see in the pages of this book.

We will show you from scriptures, all the pieces of the puzzle. It is now revealed because it was sealed and preserved for this terminal generation.

Daniel was told it would be unlocked for the end time saints to understand, but the wicked would never receive it or understand it. It is for the chosen remnant. It is not taught—it is caught. The wicked can read it, see it, and yet they will never perceive it. It is rigged for the wise (Maskilim) to understand by divine revelation.

> "Many shall be purified, and made white, and tried; but the wicked shall do wickedly: and none of the wicked shall understand; but the wise shall understand." [132]

The question to ask the skeptic is, "Why would God say, in His infallible Word, that the wise (Maskilim) men will understand and instruct many, if God is not going to reveal it?" Why would Jesus say, "Whoso readeth let him understand". After the reader sees the Abomination of Desolation stand at the Holy Place in Jerusalem, he will clearly understand Daniel's sealed prophecy.

The sealed riddle of the ages will be understood as God promised. The Abomination of Desolation is the matrix to understanding the prophetic Messianic clock to doomsday. Regardless of the popular false assumptions that no one can know when the end will come, the Apostle Paul says, "Ye are all the children of light, and the children of the day: we are not of the night, nor of darkness, that that day would come as a thief." [133]

Jesus gave us the necessary information to decode the sealed message, so that we may know when the end will come.

Sadly, the devil has been engineering a grand scheme to keep the church ignorant through disinformation and misinformation. He wants God's children to remain ignorant, even though the Abomination of Desolation is already standing in Israel, on Temple Mount, in the Holy Place, as spoken by the Prophet Daniel.

The devil is ignorant that we know when his end is coming. The matrix of the end has been decoded. We are living in a glorious time. The time of the end has been revealed, as predicted in the Holy Scriptures. The Abomination of Desolation (the Dome of the Rock) already stands at the Holy Place. Most of mankind has seen it, but they simply do not know what it is. The sealed message of Daniel reveals it. The Dome of the Rock was built at the preset time.

THIS GENERATION WILL UNDERSTAND
DANIEL'S SEALED MESSAGE

There is no doubt that God wants to dispel from you the confusing morass of false and bizarre interpretations of Biblical prophecy based upon human assumptions. The seal has been broken by the revelation given by Jesus to His disciples. We share with you straightforward prophecy from His Word, as easy to understand as God intended it to be, only for this terminal generation. He is not a God of confusion, but a God of order.

Gabriel was sent to make Daniel understand the mystery, not to confuse him, but to explain it to him. He did not change it, but simply concealed it as he received it for the wise to unveil in the Last Days, when they see the Abomination of Desolation stand in the Holy Place. It is suppose to be understood at the appointed time. All the puzzle pieces have been provided to enable us to have a complete picture.

God wants His children to prepare for our day as Noah prepared for his day. Noah knew the timeline. He was told how to prepare for his future. Biblical prophecy gives us clear end time perspective on the events in our future—the last days. As predicted by Daniel, the fourth beast is alive and well today, and the New World Order, comprised of ten economic regions, is (behind the scenes) being formed to rule the world. The cashless society is being established.

The biochip implant is already being used. The international Quartet (the United States, Russia, the European Union and the United Nations) is currently negotiating the peace treaty of which the book of Daniel speaks.

The Middle East revolution is setting the stage for the end game. You can know the headlines of tomorrow. You can escape from the ominous events that wait this terminal generation.

The Bible gives us solid evidence that these are the last days, and an exact prerecorded timetable has now been decoded for the wise to understand. Time after time, the Bible has correctly prophesied events that have occurred when God said they would. Anyone who seeks the truth cannot deny His precedents. All of God's forecasts have happened on time and in the predicted sequence.

We can trust the God who holds the future, to tell us the truth about what is coming, just as He did in the past. The Abomination of Desolation was set up exactly when Daniel predicted, in the sealed timeline he received from Gabriel.

There is an amazing correlation of current world events and the events predicted in scripture to happen in the last days. The stage is set, and the end game has begun. The countdown from the erection of the Abomination of Desolation to zero hours is impending as revealed in the Daniel timeline. The Abomination of Desolation was set on Temple Mount in Jerusalem, at the preset time in Daniel's prophecy, as we will see in the pages of this book.

It is often asked how we can know beyond a shadow of a doubt that the Bible gives us a clear timeline, leading to an historic deadline that is not shrouded in mystery? Some ask, "Shouldn't we pay attention to the fact that all past attempts to decipher the Biblical time code failed?" Others ask, "Isn't it delusional to think that after 4,000 years of failure, we should continue trying to decode the divine time cryptogram?"

We give you the answer God gave Daniel: it will be decoded in the last days, when we see the Abomination of Desolation spoken of by the Prophet Daniel. It will be revealed in our day. God said it. That settles the argument. The wise in our generation "will understand and instruct many," [134] as I have pointed out previously.

The Apostle Paul further confirms that the end time generation will decipher the Daniel Messianic Clock when he wrote, "But ye, brethren, are not in darkness, *that that day should overtake you as a thief.*" [135]

CHAPTER TEN

THE GABRIEL MESSIANIC CLOCK: FROM CYRUS' DECREE TO JESUS' CRUCIFIXION—483 YEARS UNVEILED

THE FIRST DECREE TO RESTORE JERUSALEM AND THE FIRST ADVENT OF CHRIST

In the last chapter of Daniel, the angel Gabriel tells Daniel the rest of the Messianic clock time period to doomsday. The Cyrus decree initiated the period from the return from Babylonian exile to the first advent of Christ, and His death on the cross. This prediction was actualized on time, as we have seen. God is a date setter. He keeps His preset appointments.

Gabriel gave Daniel a timeline from Cyrus' decree to restore Jerusalem, to the crucifixion of Christ:

> "Know therefore and understand, *that* from the going forth of the command to restore and build Jerusalem until Messiah the Prince, *there shall be* seven weeks and sixty-two weeks; the street shall be built again, and the wall even in troublesome times. And after the sixty-two weeks Messiah shall be cut off, but not for Himself; and the people of the prince who is to come shall destroy the city and the sanctuary. The end of it *shall be* with a flood, and till the end of the war desolations are determined." [136]

According to the Babylonian calendar, on Tashritu (October) 16, 539 B.C., Babylon fell to Medo Persia. Cyrus made a decree to restore Jerusalem, as Gabriel had foretold to Daniel. This literally happened. We have historical evidence of this prediction being fulfilled. An archaeological discovery of this proclamation was made in the Persian archives. The proclamation liberated Jews to return to their homeland and rebuild the Temple.

It is important to note that the restoration of the Jews back to Jerusalem was a prerequisite for the first advent of the Messiah. Daniel was clearly told that from the time Cyrus decreed the restoration of

Jerusalem, it would be exactly 69 weeks of years, or 483 years until Messiah would be cut off. Jesus was crucified in 30 A.D., exactly 483 years, after Cyrus' decree. The period was precise. He was cut off at the appointed time revealed to Daniel.

The timeline was specific and literal. There was a concrete fulfillment at the preset time. The Gabriel Messianic Clock timeline is not figurative it is actual and real. It is inerrant and infallible.

Gabriel pinpoints that after the first advent of Christ, there will be another major signpost before the end of days. It will be the erection of the Abomination of Desolation at the Holy Place.

THE GABRIEL MESSIANIC CLOCK: FROM THE DESTRUCTION OF THE SOLOMONIC TEMPLE TO THE BUILDING OF THE DOME OF THE ROCK ABOMINATION OF DESOLATION—1,290 YEARS

The Dome of the Rock is the "Abomination of Desolation" spoken of by the prophet Daniel. It is the revealer of the mystery of the end of time, which has been hidden through the ages. It is the final marker of time. It is a signpost on the time map. It is the epicenter of the endgame. It is the trigger of the battle of Armageddon and global terrorism. It was erected at the preset time revealed in the book of Daniel. It reveals without ambiguity the date when the world will come to an end, as we are given how many years will be left from the erection of the Dome of the Rock to calculate.

> "And from the time *that* the daily *sacrifice* is taken away,
> and the abomination of desolation is set up, *there shall be*
> one thousand two hundred and ninety days." [137]

Gabriel told Daniel that the second period must be calculated from the cessation of sacrifices when Nebuchadnezzar destroyed the First Temple (on the ninth of Av, 600 B.C.), and the daily sacrifices ceased to be offered. He told him "from the time *that* the daily *sacrifice* was taken away, and the abomination of desolation is set up, *there shall be* one thousand two hundred and ninety days."

This is the event to which Jesus referred when he said, "When ye therefore shall see the abomination of desolation, spoken of by Daniel the prophet, stand in the holy place, (whoso readeth, let him understand)." [138] The Daniel timeline to doomsday is calculated from that event. The Dome of the Rock was erected in 691 A.D. the period is so exact, factoring in the year zero. (600 + 1290 years = 691 A.D. add year zero)

The period was definitive, and the starting point specific: the cessation of sacrifices. God is a date setter. He is not the author of confusion. His Messianic calendar is clear.

The Dome of the Rock was built precisely at the preset time revealed to Daniel. This is why Jesus said, "when you see the abomination of desolation standing at the holy place." Those who read Daniel's timeline will then understand because "blessed is he that waits and comes to one thousand three hundred and thirty five" to the end of days. (691 A.D. + 1335 years = 2026 A.D.).

In contrast to man's prognostications, there are no discrepancies in Biblical chronology. The Gabriel Messianic Clock is confirmed by extra-Biblical evidence. The date the Dome of the Rock was erected is documented. The period from the cessation of sacrifices after the Babylonian destruction of the Solomonic Temple to the building of the Abomination of Desolation is exactly 1,290 years, as predicted by Daniel the Prophet.

The Messianic calendar given to Daniel by Gabriel is not Biblical mumbo jumbo or a mystical celestial time enigma not to be understood. It is a straightforward simple concrete timeline. It is anchored in a historical event recorded in history. It is solid, factual and irrefutable.

The Dome of the Rock is referred to as the Abomination of Desolation, because it constitutes the cause of the coming all out war against Israel by the Islamic hordes to liberate Jerusalem and Temple Mount. Jerusalem is the epicenter of the coming conflict, and Temple Mount is ground zero. The Abomination of Desolation stands at the Holy Place today. The whole Islamic world is preparing to go to war over Temple Mount, as foretold by Gabriel.

On October 22, 1988, in El Nur, the following quote appeared:

> "We wait for the moment when all the Jews will gather in Palestine and that will be the greatest day for enormous massacre."

The cause of the coming enormous massacre, in Hebrew, is *"shiqqutzim shomem,"* the Abomination of Desolation. In the New Testament, *"bdelugma"* is an abomination or a detestable object of horror. The Islamic world will fight for the control of Temple Mount, to protect the *"bdelugma"*, the Dome of the Rock. Gabriel calls it the Abomination of Desolation because it is going to cause the desolation of the modern state of Israel. It was erected at the preset time, 1290 years from the cessation of sacrifices in 600 B.C.

> "Therefore when you see the 'Abomination of Desolation,' spoken of by Daniel the prophet, standing in the holy place" (whoever reads, let him understand)." [139]

Jesus said that when we see the "Abomination of Desolation" stand at the Holy Place, those who read prophecy should understand the Daniel timeline to doomsday, since the calculation to the end of time is marked from that event.

The reason we know that the Gabriel Messianic Clock to doomsday is reliable and accurate is because it never failed. The period from Cyrus' decree to the crucifixion of Jesus was fulfilled at the appointed time.

The period from the cessation of sacrifices after the destruction of the First Temple by Nebuchadnezzar, to the Abomination of Desolation was again fulfilled at the preset time. These timelines were given hundreds of years before they were fulfilled, in each case, literally, physically, naturally and concretely, at the predetermined time revealed to Daniel. Gabriel's Messianic Clock has been proven infallible.

Gabriel told Daniel that there would be two specific periods to calculate to the blessedness of the Messianic kingdom. The first would be 1,290 years from when he witnessed the cessation of sacrifices in 600 B.C. The second period will be 1,335 years from the erection of the Dome of the Rock to the Kingdom. A total of 2,625 years from 600 B.C.

> "And from the time *that* the daily *sacrifice was* taken away, and the Abomination of Desolation is set up, *there shall be* one thousand two hundred and ninety days. Blessed *is* he who waits, and comes to the one thousand three hundred and thirty-five days." [140]

Gabriel revealed to Daniel the timeline to the Messianic Kingdom.

MESSIANIC CLOCK

DESTRUCTION OF THE SOLOMONIC TEMPLE TO THE BUILDING OF THE DOME OF THE ROCK / ABOMINATION OF DESOLATION: 1,290 YEARS

600 B.C.	Destruction of First Temple and the Cessation of Sacrifices	2 Chronicles 36:19 Daniel 12:11
539 B.C.	The Rise of Medo-Persia	Daniel 5:30
450 B.C.	Cyrus' Decree to Restore Jerusalem 69 weeks of years or 483 years before Crucifixion of Christ	Daniel 9:25-26 Matthew 27
334 B.C.	The Rise of Greece	Daniel 8:21
63 B.C.	The Rise of Rome	Daniel 7:23
4 B.C.	Jesus Christ is Born	Matthew 1,2
30 A.D.	Jesus Christ is Crucified 483 years from Cyrus' Decree as Predicted by the Prophet Daniel	Luke 23
70 A.D.	Jerusalem Destroyed by Titus	Matthew 24: 1-2
691 A.D.	The Abomination of Desolation, the Dome of the Rock, Erected on Temple Mount 1,290 Years from the Cessation of Sacrifices in 600 B.C. (600 B.C. + 1,290 years = 691 A.D. (add the year zero) precision timing	Daniel 9:26, 12:11 Matthew 24:15

The code breaker is the Abomination of Desolation. "When ye therefore shall see the abomination of desolation, spoken of by Daniel the prophet, stand in the holy place, (whoso readeth, let him understand:) Matthew 24:15

CHAPTER ELEVEN

THE MESSIANIC CLOCK: FROM THE DOME OF THE ROCK TO DOOMSDAY—1,335 YEARS UNVEILED

Daniel wanted to know earth's ultimate expiration date, "the end of these wonders." Gabriel went ahead and gave him a sequential development leading to the end of time. He began from the fall of Jerusalem and the cessation of sacrifices, to the crucifixion of Jesus, to the end of the time of the Gentiles, the battle of Armageddon, and finally the Advent of the glorious Messianic Kingdom.

Gabriel told Daniel how long it would take from the last signpost, the erection of the Dome of the Rock, to the end of time.

> "And from the time that the daily sacrifice *was* taken away, and the abomination of desolation is set up, there shall be one thousand two hundred and ninety days. Blessed is he who waits, and comes to the one thousand three hundred and thirty-five days." [141]

The erection in 691 A.D. of the Dome of the Rock (the Abomination of Desolation) marks the beginning of the last period that will conclude with the consummation of history. The Abomination of Desolation was a pivotal event that signaled the commencement of the last 1,335 years of history, leading to the blessed advent of the Messiah at the end of that period. This is why Jesus said, "when you see the Abomination of Desolation" let the reader understand the timeline since the remaining years to doomsday are given. *"Blessed is he who waits, and comes to the one thousand three hundred and thirty-five days."* [142]

The tabulation of 1,335 years from the Abomination of Desolation calculates the termination date to be on Rosh Hashanah, Tishri 1, in the Jewish year of 5788. This date corresponds to the Julian calendar date of (691 A.D. + 1335 years = 2026 A.D.) October 2, 2026 A.D. when 1,335 years expires. It is the same time that the Genesis time template and the Noahian time template expires. Amazing precision timing.

The Gabriel Messianic Clock is precise and accurate. History has proved time and again the Messianic calendar to be inerrant. It has never failed. There are only 14 years left before time expires. However, Jesus said that the Gabriel Messianic Clock timeline would be cut short.

> "And unless those days were shortened, no flesh would be saved; but for the elect's sake those days will be shortened." [143]

We stand today in the face of the greatest prophetic fulfillment: the end of time as we know it. In the years that lie ahead of us, we are about to see major prophetic events of apocalyptic proportion, unparalleled in history. We have gone beyond the point of no return. Perilous times are fast approaching. Gabriel described the coming worldwide catastrophe scheduled to occur in our generation with these ominous words:

> "At that time Michael shall stand up, the great prince who stands *watch* over the sons of your people; *and there shall be a time of trouble, such as never was since there was a nation, even to that time.* And at that time your people shall be delivered, everyone who is found written in the book." [144]

Our greatest tragedy is the facts that mainstream Christianity is asleep at the wheel, while mankind is descending into the abyss with no warning. Satan is going to wreak havoc on the unprepared church. Big government, big business and big religion are merging into a marriage of convenience.

The church has become the catalyst of the New World Order. We are living through the greatest apostasy of the church since the time of Jesus. The church is lost in a lost world. There are very few truly prophetic voices left. In today's world, sadly, most are prophets for profit.

The beleaguered masses will perish, clinging to false religiosity and false hope from the pulpits of our churches. Most church attendees are told that nobody knows when the end will come. Scripture refutes this:

> "Many shall be purified, made white, and refined, but the wicked shall do wickedly; and none of the wicked shall understand, *but the wise shall understand.*" [145]

History has authenticated as accurate and irreversible the Messianic clock given to Daniel. The epic drama of the ages is about to begin: nations, peoples, every tribe and tongue, and celestial players are all about to take their place in the end game of our day—the last of the last days.

The end of days encoded in the Gabriel calculations is about to play out. The foretold Biblical time template chronicled in the distant past 28 centuries ago, gives the headlines of tomorrow! The implications of these predictions for this present generation are both shocking and perilous.

In the Jewish Talmud Avodad Zarah, page 9a states that the world will exist for 6,000 years from creation. The Gabriel Messianic Clock terminates exactly and precisely at the end of 6,000 years from creation. The Acharit Hayhmin, or end of days, is in our immediate future.

The period is exact and precise. It correlates with Daniel's timetable, given to him by Gabriel. The Gabriel Messianic Clock establishes Rosh Hashanah, Tishri I, 4026 B.C. as the first day of creation and the dawn of time. It is exactly six thousand years from creation to the Gabriel Messianic Clock doomsday. Only God could establish such a precise timeline. This synchronization is of monumental importance, as it reveals the divine architect of the Messianic Clock given to Daniel.

THE DANIEL MESSIANIC CLOCK:
DESTRUCTION OF THE FIRST TEMPLE TO DOOMSDAY

Year	Event	Scripture
600 B.C.	Destruction and Cessation of Sacrifices from the First Temple	2 Chronicles 36:19
450 B.C.	Cyrus' Decree to Restore Jerusalem	Ezekiel 1:1 – 3
30 A.D.	The Crucifixion of Christ Exactly 483 years from 450 B.C.	Daniel 9:26 Mark 15:25 – 26
691 A.D.	The Abomination of Desolation / End of 1,290 years from the Cessation of the Sacrifices from the First Temple	Daniel 12:11 Matthew 24:15
1536 A.D.	Suleiman The Magnificent's Second Decree to Restore Jerusalem	Daniel 9:25 – 26
2012 A.D.	The Beginning of the 69th Week of Daniel from Second Decree to Restore Jerusalem	Daniel 9:25
2019 A.D.	The Beginning of the 70th Week of Daniel	Daniel 9:24
2026 A.D.	Rosh Hashanah/ Doomsday The End of 1,335 years from 691 A.D.	Daniel 12:12

Rosh Hashanah/New Year comes in the fall
The dates used align Jewish year with the Julian calendar

CHAPTER TWELVE

THE GABRIEL MESSIANIC CLOCK: FROM THE SECOND DECREE BY SULEIMAN THE MAGNIFICENT TO RESTORE JERUSALEM TO DOOMSAY—490 YEARS UNVEILED

The future is designed to follow the Biblical types and shadows. The past gives us the blueprint of the future Messianic Clock. Everything in history is predestined to follow the historical prototype.

The first decree issued by Cyrus to restore Jerusalem initiated the preset period of 483 years to the crucifixion of Jesus. The first decree ended the Babylonian exile, and lasted until 70 A.D., when Titus destroyed Jerusalem the second time. The Jews were scattered all over the world for over 1,900 years, until 1948 A.D.

In 1536 A.D., Suleiman the Magnificent, issued the second decree to restore Jerusalem. He built the wall of Jerusalem. This was the exact time predicted by Gabriel in the Messianic Clock for the second decree to restore Jerusalem. This second decree established the last cycle of judgment before the Messianic Kingdom. There are two exiles, two returns, and two decrees. The period initiated by the first decree would be 69 weeks of years to the first coming of Christ when he will be cut off or crucified.

"Know therefore and understand, that from the going forth of the command to restore and build Jerusalem until Messiah the Prince, there shall be seven weeks and sixty-two weeks; The street shall be built again, and the wall Even in troublesome times. And after the sixty-two weeks Messiah shall be cut off, but not for Himself; and the people of the prince who is to come shall destroy the city and the sanctuary. The end of it shall be with a flood, and till the end of the war desolations are determined." [146]

The 70 shabuwas were decreed from the second decree to restore Jerusalem to bring in everlasting righteousness, to seal up the vision and prophecy. The end of 490 years from the Suleiman decree culminates with the return of the Messiah to establish everlasting righteousness. (1536 A.D. +490 years = 2026 A.D.)

> "Seventy 'sevens' are decreed for your people and your holy city to finish transgression, to put an end to sin, to atone for wickedness, to bring in everlasting righteousness, to seal up vision and prophecy and to anoint the Most Holy Place". [147]

The second decree, by Suleiman the Magnificent, 1536 A.D. marks the countdown of the last 490 years before the end of time. Its termination on October 2, 2026, happens also to be precisely the same termination of 1,335 years from the erection of the Dome of the Rock in 691 A.D., Rosh Hashanah 5788 Jewish year, October 2, 2026.

> "Blessed *is* he who waits, and comes to the one thousand three hundred and thirty-five days." [148]

The seventy sevens calculates to the exact point in history as established in the Genesis time template, the Noahian time template and the end of 1,335 years from the Dome of the Rock to the end of days.

As the first decree by Cyrus calculated to the First Advent of the Messiah, the second decree by Suleiman the Magnificent will calculate to the Second Advent of Christ "to bring in everlasting righteousness and to seal up the vision and prophecy and anoint the Most Holy".

God's timetable is cyclical. In 1536 B.C., the Angel of the Lord appeared to Moses to command him to lead the children of Israel out of Egyptian slavery to go to the Promised Land. In 1536 A.D. Rabbi Caro was told by an angel to go to Eretz Yisrael. He returned and built the city of Safed. Since that time, Jewish people from all over the world have been returning to build the foundation of the modern state of Israel.

The year 1536 A.D. was a pivotal year, Suleiman the Magnificent signed the second decree to restore Jerusalem, He rebuilt the Jerusalem wall. September 17, 2012 is the beginning of the 69th week of years from the time. It marks the "beginning of sorrows", "for nation will rise against nation, and kingdom against kingdom. And there will be earthquakes in various places, and there will be famines and troubles." [149]

The political explosion in the Middle East, economic meltdown and financial upheaval in the capital markets are all part of the conditions necessary for the rise of the New World Order. This new World order will initiate global tyranny by the Antichrist, the son of perdition. He is alive and well today. As you read this book, he is somewhere on Planet earth.

The preset time window for his rise to power is in the last two sabbatical seven-year cycles. The last cycle leads to the end of time on the Gabriel Messianic Clock, Rosh Hashanah, of the Jewish year 5788, which corresponds to the Julian calendar year of October 2, 2026 A.D.

By following the broad cyclical pattern of Biblical chronology that has been established throughout six thousand years of written history, we find another clue. Solomon began to lay the foundation of the First Temple 480 years after the conquest and division of the land among the twelve tribes. Could this be a blueprint for the Third Temple from 1536 A.D. exactly 480 years from Suleiman's decree to restore Jerusalem.

It is important to note that Jesus began His ministry 480 years after the issuing of Cyrus' decree to restore Jerusalem. It is no coincidence that 480 years from Suleiman's decree also happens to be the 50th year (Jubilee) after the liberation of Temple Mount by Israel in 1967, Jewish reckoning. It also happens to be 100th anniversary (2 Jubilees) of the 1917 liberation of "Palestine" from the Ottoman Empire.

This Biblical pattern was established from the first return and the time template for the second return from the Diaspora. The second return began in 1948. It took seven extra years after the first return, before work began on the Second Temple.

On Rosh Hashanah of the 78th year from the Babylonian holocaust and destruction of the temple sacrifices were restored. Since the rebirth of Israel, on Rosh Hashanah 5788 Jewish year, (Julian year October 2,

2026) it's the 78th year, and it correlates exactly with the cleansing of the Temple 78 years after the beginning of Babylonian destruction and exile. The pattern is exact: 1) to finish the transgression and to make an end of sin; 2) to make reconciliation of iniquity; 3) to bring in everlasting righteousness; 4) to seal up the vision and prophecy; 5) to anoint the Most Holy. It is exactly the end of the 70 (shabuwas) or 490 years from Suleiman the Magnificent decree to "bring in everlasting righteousness."

A careful examination of the Biblical cyclical pattern makes the 480th year from the Suleiman decree a critical year in the prophetic calendar. The 69th week of Daniel begins September 17, 2012. From this point on, it will be extremely interesting to watch the events on Temple Mount. The prophetic epicenter of the end game is Temple Mount. The spotlight is already being focused on Jerusalem and Temple Mount, particularly in regards to the current peace negotiations.

The Biblical prophecy makes it clear that the coming battle of Armageddon is going to be over Jerusalem and Temple Mount.

It is predicted by Zechariah the prophet how Jerusalem will be a source of conflict in the last days.

> "The Lord, who stretches out the heavens, who lays the foundation of the earth, and who forms the human spirit within a person, declares: "I am going to make Jerusalem a cup that sends all the surrounding peoples reeling. Judah will be besieged as well as Jerusalem. On that day, when all the nations of the earth are gathered against her, I will make Jerusalem an immovable rock for all the nations. All who try to move it will injure themselves." [150]

Antichrist will move to Jerusalem as his capital. He will reign as the final chapter of the legacy of Satan's rebellion of his government against God. He will be the manifestation of the mystery of iniquity, which has been at work among man for centuries. Finally Satan personified in the person of the Antichrist will rule this earth.

The present global configurations and commotions are a prelude to Satan's takeover of this world's leadership. He will rule from the Third Temple in Jerusalem on Temple Mount, pretending to be god. He will cause horrendous persecutions of the saints who reject his claim to be god.

The Antichrist will lead the nations into the battle of Armageddon to exterminate the Jews and to take control of Jerusalem. The battle will be consummated by the glorious parousia, or coming of the Lord Jesus Christ to rescue Jerusalem and to deliver the nations from Satan's domination.

Based upon clear scriptures, "all Israel will be saved". [151] They will be born again, saved and sanctified. "And the Lord their God shall save them in that day as the flock of his people." [152] The dead Jewish saints will be raised from the dead; "many of them that sleep in the dust of the earth shall be raised, some to everlasting life and some to shame and everlasting contempt". [153] The wicked will be raised one thousand years later after the millennium rule of Christ, during the second resurrection unto everlasting contempt.

"But the rest of the dead did not live again until the thousand years were finished. This *is* the first resurrection. Blessed and holy *is* he who has part in the first resurrection. Over such the second death has no power, but they shall be priests of God and of Christ, and shall reign with Him a thousand years." [154]

"And I saw the dead, small and great, standing before God, and books were opened. And another book was opened, which is *the Book* of Life. And the dead were judged according to their works, by the things which were written in the books." [155]

"And anyone not found written in the Book of Life was cast into the lake of fire." [156]

Finally Israel's Messianic hope will be fulfilled. They will be delivered by their Messiah from extermination and saved. What a glorious hope. When the Prince of Peace rules from Jerusalem there will finally be peace on earth.

The Gabriel Messianic Clock predicts all these things to take place during the 69th and 70th "weeks" spoken of in Daniel: September 17, 2012 to October 2, 2026. The last 490 years, or 70 shabuwas time span, from the Suleiman's decree in 1536 A.D., to Rosh Hashanah on October 2, 2026 A.D. (Julian calendar) when the Daniel Messianic Clock ends.

This generation has been told what lies ahead before it takes place. In this decade the Jews will build the Third Temple. This provision will be part of the current "road map" negotiations. The journey began with Solomon, the Third King of Israel, building the First Temple in 1026 B.C. This was a magnificent structure that took 14 years to complete, and the glory of God filled this Temple. Nebuchadnezzar destroyed the Temple built during Solomon's reign in 600 B.C.

The Second Temple was built by the Jewish exiles after their return from Babylon. King Herod expanded and beautified the Second Temple. He began to renovate the Temple in 19 B.C. The main structure took 10 years, yet he continued the work until 64 A.D. Six years later it was destroyed by Titus, to complete the suppression of the Jewish revolt. The Second Temple was destroyed in 70 A.D.

A new chapter is about to begin. According to the Gabriel Messianic Clock, the Third Temple will be built in these last days on Temple Mount, opposite the Dome of the Rock. It is referred to as Ezekiel's Temple. He wrote about it while in exile in Babylon. He had a vision in which he saw a glorious temple with a wall around it to protect the worshipers.

Prophet (Nabi) Ezekiel saw the Dome of the Rock next to it and he called it the "profane thing". Ezekiel was instructed to measure the protective wall between the Dome of the Rock and the Jewish Temple. "He measured it by the four sides: it had a wall about five hundred reeds long, and five hundred broad, to make a separation between the Temple and the profane thing." [157] (The Dome of the Rock)

The book of Revelation also describes the coming Third Temple on Mount Moriah (Temple Mount). John goes further and pinpoints that the Dome of the Rock stands at the court of the Gentiles, or the Holy Place. He was also told to measure the coming Third Temple on Temple Mount. This is how he describes his vision of the Third Temple, as God shows him what it will look like when it is built shortly before the end of time.

> "Then I was given a reed like a measuring rod. And the angel stood saying, "Rise and measure the Temple of God, the altar and those who worship there. But leave out the court, which is outside the Temple, and do not measure it, for it has been given to the Gentiles. And they will tread the Holy city underfoot for 42 months." [158]

The court of the Gentiles is where the Dome of the Rock stands. Two worship places will stand side-by-side within the next 14 years, one as the Abomination of Desolation, spoken of by the prophet Daniel, and the Third Temple. The Dome of the Rock (the profane thing, the Abomination of Desolation) will remain in the hands of Islam, during the short time of the erection of the Third Temple, before Messiah comes with the Millennium Temple.

The ancient predictions give us the news headlines of tomorrow, and a preview of the peace accord being negotiated right now by the leaders of the Security Council and the Quartet. As part of the Peace Agreement, Israel will be granted the right to worship on Temple Mount.

We will soon see this whole prophetic event take place in our day. The Jews will build a wall around their worship place next to the Dome of the Rock, to protect themselves from Islamic extremists. The Third Temple will bring spiritual renewal to the Jewish people all over the world. It will be a place filled with the glory of God, as Ezekiel saw it in his vision. Great days lie ahead for Israel, in the midst of increasing tension in the region.

It is interesting to note that 70 years after the Babylonian Holocaust, Israel returned to build the Second Temple. Could it be that 70 years after the Holocaust by Hitler, Israel will build the Third Temple?

PARALLELISM BETWEEN CHRIST'S AND ANTICHRIST TIMELINE

The sixty-ninth week of Daniel marks the beginning of the Messianic era the cosmic battle has already begun. We are in transition from the age of the church to the age of the Kingdom. End time prophecies are unfolding before our eyes in a mind-boggling way. What we are seeing is beyond the realm of coincidence, unfathomable predictions being fulfilled with unquestionable reliability and credibility. Seeing these ancient prophecies being fulfilled carries a heavy responsibility. In the face of such overwhelming evidence of colossal events foretold of old happening every day with amazing specificity, should alert the saints of the challenges that lie ahead in this decade of destiny. It is time to get red hot for Jesus and prepare to meet our God.

What is apparent from history is that Jesus began His ministry during the middle of the sixty-ninth week of years from the signing of the Cyrus decree to restore Jerusalem, exactly 480 years. He was crucified rose again, ascended to the right hand of God at the end of the sixty-ninth week of Daniel. It is possible that the Antichrist, as a copycat, will begin his reign of terror 480 years from the signing of Suleiman the Magnificent's Decree to restore Jerusalem in 1536 A.D., which would make the year 2016 pivotal.

Jesus healed the sick: Antichrist will kill the saints. Jesus cleansed the Second Temple at the end of the sixty-ninth week of Daniel: Antichrist will defile the Third Temple. Jesus invited people to worship God in spirit and truth: the Antichrist will force people to worship him.

It is clear from scriptures that major prophetic events are preset to happen in this decade. As Christ ascended to heaven at the end of the sixty-ninth week of Daniel from the Cyrus decree, could it be that He will descend from heaven at the end of the sixty-ninth week from Suleiman Magnificent's Decree, to rapture the saints? You cannot help but see an emerging pattern and the connection between His first Advent and His Second Advent.

Gabriel is very specific regarding the two decrees, the two comings of Christ and two sets of periods from the issuing of the decrees to restore Jerusalem. Gabriel clearly says at the end of the period calculated from the first decree the Messiah would be cut off. The second decree would lead to the second coming of the Messiah the Prince in Glory and Power. He said,

> "Seventy weeks are determined for your people and for your holy city, to finish the transgression, to make an end of sins, to make reconciliation for iniquity, to bring in everlasting righteousness, to seal up vision and prophecy, and to anoint the Most Holy." [159]

The second decree by Suleiman the Magnificent initiated the second period of 70 shabuwas 490 years that will culminate in the Advent of the Messianic kingdom to finish the transgression, to make an end of sins to make reconciliation for iniquity, to bring in everlasting righteousness, to seal up vision and prophecy and anoint the most Holy.

There is an impeccable parallelism between Jesus first coming and second. As He fought the devil after his baptism for 40 days immediately after the dispensation of the law, He will return immediately after the dispensation of grace to fight against the devil, the Antichrist and the False prophet. He will cast the Antichrist and the False prophet into the lake of fire and bind the devil for a thousand years. All these momentous events will take place in these final earth days.

The end of the second period aligns with the end of 1,335 years preset to the end of time from the erection of the Abomination of Desolation (The Dome of the Rock), the end of the Genesis time template and the Noahian time template. No human could have ever envisioned these two decrees to restore Jerusalem and the two comings of the Messiah. What is clear is that the seventieth week of Daniel marks the end of time.

This is going to be a decade of troublesome times until the end. Gabriel painted a grim picture of distress of nations, insurrections, commotions, wars, turmoil and rumors of wars. The birth pangs, a world in travail, as foretold, "there will be a time of distress such as never occurred since there was a nation until that time." [160] It is going to be the greatest distress in scope and magnitude. We are going where no other generation has ever gone. It is obvious from Gabriel's statement.

The present conditions in our world constitute the countdown and the setting of the stage for the collapse of Wall Street and Main Street, the demise and the collapse of the USA as a sole super power, the collapse of nation states, collapse of global banking and financial capital markets and global social upheaval.

The pathway that our generation is on is leading to global conflict and nuclear holocaust as nations fight for dwindling natural resources. The present global catastrophic events are destined to collapse global civilization, create pandemics caused by biological warfare, contamination of global water sources and death of marine life on land and at sea, global food shortage and lack of clean water and crop failure due to nuclear winter.

As if it were not enough, contemporaneous to these perilous events the Bible says there will be unprecedented natural disasters, major earthquakes, tsunamis, radiation from solar flares, falling comets, the sun will be darkened, the moon will turn into blood and the powers of the heavens will be shaken.

The New World Order will rise headed by the Antichrist a false Messiah. He will offer false peace to the world. He will demand that every human being be bio-chipped with 666 or face death.

We stand today at the threshold of the darkest days in the history of the world and the beginning of the countdown to Armageddon.

THE MESSIANIC CLOCK: SECOND DECREE TO RESTORE JERUSALEM TO THE NEW JERUSALEM – 490 YEARS DECREED

Year	Event	Scripture
1536 A.D.	Suleiman the Magnificent's Decree to Restore Jerusalem 70 week decreed (490 years)	Daniel 9:24
1917 A.D.	Liberation of Palestine and Jerusalem from Ottoman Empire as the First Plane Flew over Jerusalem	Isaiah 31:5
1947 A.D.	Partition of the Holy Land	Joel 3:1-2
1948 A.D.	The Rebirth of Israel	Isaiah 6:6-8 Isaiah 11:11-12 Ezekiel 36:24
1967 A.D.	Temple Mount Restored to the Jewish People	Revelations 11:12 Ezekiel 42:16-20
1991 A.D.	The Collapse of the Former Soviet Union for Denying Jews Exit Visas	Isaiah 43:6
1995 A.D	The Rabin Peace Accords	Daniel 9:27
2012 – 2019 A.D.	The 69th week of Daniel from the Signing of the Second Decree to Restore Jerusalem	Daniel 9:25-26
2019 – 2026 A.D.	The 70th Week of Daniel 483 Years from Second Decree	Daniel 9:24
2026 A.D.	Rosh Hashanah, Tishri 1 End of Days 490 years from the Second Decree	Revelations 10:7 Revelations 16:17

CHAPTER THIRTEEN

GABRIEL MESSIANIC CLOCK: FROM THE CONFIRMATION
OF THE ISRAELI PEACE TREATY TO DOOMSDAY—7 YEARS

Rosh Hashanah, September 17, 2012, is the beginning of the 69th "week" foretold by Daniel, and is calculated from the date of Suleiman the Magnificent's Decree to restore Jerusalem. This is the preset initial phase of Antichrist's dispensation, or the beginning of his rise to power. We have reached the predicted 2012-2026 A.D. historic time window in which the son of perdition (Antichrist) emerges as a world leader, according to the ancient predictions by Daniel anytime within the time window.

Biblical prophecy gives us the profile of the Antichrist and identifies the political, social and economic mega-trends that will shape our impending path to the New World Order, which leads to the end of days.

The prophet Daniel calls the Antichrist the little horn "that waxed exceeding great towards the south and towards the east and towards the pleasant land." [161] The Antichrist will establish one worldwide government, and he will have insane hatred for Christians and Jews. He will attempt to exterminate both groups. He will unleash the greatest tribulation of the people of God in human history. He is the personification of Satan. He is consumed with indignation against the Jewish people, since Jesus came from the tribe of Judah to save the world.

The Bible calls this period "Jacob's trouble." [162] According to the book of revelation, this evil global tyrant, arrogant and impious, will persecute anyone who refuses to worship him and take his number 666. We now know that this procedure is possible using biochip implants.

> "So they worshiped the dragon who gave authority to the beast; and they worshiped the beast, saying, 'Who *is* like the beast? Who is able to make war with him?' And he was

given a mouth speaking great things and blasphemies, and he was given authority to continue for forty-two months.

Then he opened his mouth in blasphemy against God, to blaspheme His name, His tabernacle, and those who dwell in heaven. It was granted to him to make war with the saints and to overcome them. And authority was given him over every tribe, tongue and nation.

All who dwell on the earth will worship him, whose names have not been written in the Book of Life of the Lamb slain from the foundation of the world." [163]

The question in the heart of every person is when the Antichrist will emerge as a world leader. The prophet Daniel gives us a very definitive and specific duration of 7 years before the end of earth time, which is scheduled to occur between 2012 and 2026. He is the next major prophetic event in these days.

The coming world leader is going to endorse the current Rabin Peace Process as a solution to the Middle East crisis. Gabriel told Daniel the name Rabbim (Rabin), which translates as *many*, and identifies the treaty, which Antichrist will confirm. It is basically a modified 1967 border between Israel and the newly formed Palestinian state with some land swaps.

Gabriel was simply identifying the Jewish Prime Minister whose peace accords are the basis for the coming peace agreement. The Bible tells us that the treaty will be signed as a seven-year agreement. It is specific about the Rabin Peace Accords and definitive in its predictions regarding the duration of the agreement.

The Antichrist will break the "land for peace" covenant in the middle of the seven years. He will desecrate the Third Temple by entering into the Temple and declaring himself god. He will launch an unparalleled anti-Semitic genocide against the Jews and the saints.

According to the Messianic clock, he will agree to a two state solution at the beginning, then he will betray Israel halfway through the seven-year treaty, due to Islamic pressure.

"He shall confirm a covenant with many (Rabin Peace Accord) for one week. But in the middle of the week, He shall bring an end to sacrifices and offerings, and on the wing of abomination shall be one who makes desolate even until the consummation which is determined, is poured out on the desolate." [164]

Gabriel pinpoints the time when the seven-year covenant is broken: exactly three and a half years from the signing of the document. The signing of the Peace Agreement is critical for a watcher of Bible prophecy, in order to discern the nearness of the end of days.

The ancient Nabi Daniel tells the reader when to begin calculating the seven years before it is broken. The reader will be able to predict when the Antichrist will enter the Third Temple and declare himself god: everything is revealed and prerecorded for the saints.

The New Testament describes the spiritual condition of the church during the terminal generation. The Apostle Paul warned the saints concerning the apostasy just before the manifestation of the Antichrist:

"Let no one deceive you by any means, for that day will not come unless the falling away comes first and the man of sin is revealed, the son of perdition, who opposes and exalts himself above all that is called God or that is worshipped, so that he sits as God in the (Third Temple) temple of God (on Temple Mount) showing himself that he is God. The lawless one will be revealed whom the Lord will consume with the breath of His mouth and destroy with the brightness of His coming." [165]

The coming Peace Treaty with Israel marks the beginning of the last seven years before doomsday well before 2026 A.D. The 69th week marks the pivotal appointed time.

CHAPTER FOURTEEN

THE MESSIANIC CLOCK: FIRST ADVENT TO SECOND ADVENT
2,000 YEARS UNVEILED

The Gabriel Messianic Clock pinpoints that the second Temple would be destroyed after the Messiah is cut off:

> "Know therefore and understand, *that* from the going forth of the command to restore and build Jerusalem until Messiah the Prince, *there shall be* seven weeks and sixty-two weeks; the street shall be built again, and the wall even in troublesome times. And after the sixty-two weeks Messiah shall be cut off, but not for Himself, and the *people of the prince who is to come shall destroy the city and the sanctuary.* The end of it *shall be* with a flood, and till the end of the war desolations are determined." [166]

When the Messiah visited the second Temple the last time, he wept over Jerusalem and the future of the temple, because He saw its coming destruction in 70 A.D.

> "If you had known, even you, especially in this your day, the things *that make* for now they are hidden from your eyes. For days will come upon you when your enemies will build an embankment around you, surround you and close you in on every side, and level you, and your children within you, to the ground; and they will not leave in you one stone upon another, because you did not know the time of your visitation." [167]

The Jews failed to recognize their Messiah. Though many prophecies foretold when the Messiah would come, even some of their Rabbis predicted when the Messiah would come. In the Babylonian Talmud, Rabbi Elias, who lived 200 years before Jesus, wrote:

> "The world endures six thousand years: Two thousand before the law, two thousand with the law and two thousand with the messiah." (Babylonian Talmud Sanhedrin 96 1-99a)

According to rabbinical commentary, the Messiah was to come at the end of the fourth millennium. He would then be with the people for two thousand years. He was revealed exactly four thousand years after 4026 B.C. He was baptized in 26 A.D., exactly 4,000 years from creation, as Rabbi Elias predicted. He has been with his born-again children, living in them for two thousand years, as predicted in the Babylonian Talmud Sanhedrin.

Rabbi Kaltina, in the "Babylonian Talmud Sanhedrin" 96b-99a, further reveals the millennium rule of Christ. He wrote:

> "The world endures six thousand years and one thousand it shall be laid waste. That is, the enemies of God shall be laid waste, whereof it is said, 'The Lord alone shall be exalted in that day.' As out of seven years every seventh is a year of remission, so out of seven thousand years of the world, the seventh millennium shall be the thousand years of remission, that God alone may be exalted in that day."

Babylonian Talmud also foretells that the second Temple would be destroyed. Babylonian Rabbis predicted it. They knew it was coming. They warned the future generations about it. Rabbi Joseph wrote in "The Babylonian Talmud Tractate Nazir" 32b:

> "Had I been there, I should have said to them, 'Is it not written, "The temple of the Lord, the temple of the Lord, the temple of the Lord," are these which points to [the

destruction of] the first and second temples. Granted that they knew it would be destroyed, did they know when this would occur? Rabbi Abaye objected: And did they not know when? Is it not written, 'Seventy weeks are determined upon thy people, and upon thy holy city."

The Second Temple was indeed destroyed after the Messiah was cut off and after seventy weeks of years from Cyrus' decree to restore Jerusalem.

The Messianic Clock predicts the building of the Third Temple after the second exile from the Diaspora. The sacrifices will be restored. The Antichrist will stop the sacrifices.

"And out of one of them came a little horn which grew exceedingly great toward the south, toward the east, and toward the Glorious *Land*. And it grew up to the host of heaven; and it cast down *some* of the host and *some* of the stars to the ground, and trampled them. He even exalted *himself* as high as the Prince of the host; and by him the daily *sacrifices* were taken away, and the place of His sanctuary was cast down. Because of transgression, an army was given over *to the horn* to oppose the daily *sacrifices;* and he cast truth down to the ground. He did *all this* and prospered." [168]

The Antichrist will desecrate the Third Temple after he breaks the seven-year peace treaty with Israel. He will set up the image of the beast in the Third Temple, according to the book of Revelation.

"And he deceives those who dwell on the earth by those signs which he was granted to do in the sight of the beast, telling those who dwell on the earth to make an image to the beast who was wounded by the sword and lived. He was granted *power* to give breath to the image of the beast, that the image of the beast should both speak and cause as many as would not worship the image of the beast to be killed." [169]

The exact period that the image of the beast will stand in the Holy Place in the third Temple will be 42 months before doomsday. "Then I was given a reed like a measuring rod. And the angel stood, saying, "Rise and measure the temple of God, the altar, and those who worship there. But leave out the court, which is outside the temple, and do not measure it, for it has been given to the Gentiles. And they will tread the holy city underfoot for forty-two months." [170]

During this period of three and half years there will be no more sacrifices at the Third Temple. The Antichrist will sit in the Temple declaring himself god manifest in the flesh and demanding universal worship.

The Messianic Clock is clear: one only needs to calculate three and a half years from the cessation of sacrifices to determine the end of days. The period is exact. It is given to enable the saints to know the time of the end. The devout Jews will flee Jerusalem when the Antichrist declares himself god and enters the Temple. This is the sign to begin the tabulation of three and a half years until the cleansing of the Temple, when Christ destroys the Antichrist at His coming.

"Antichrist who opposes and exalts himself above all that is called God or that is worshiped, so that he sits as God in the temple of God, showing himself that he is God. Do you not remember that when I was still with you I told you these things? And now you know what is restraining, that he may be revealed in his own time.

For the mystery of lawlessness is already at work; only He who now restrains *will do so* until He is taken out of the way. And then the lawless one will be revealed, whom the Lord will consume with the breath of His mouth and destroy with the brightness of His coming. [171]

The puzzle of the age has been solved. The saints will be able to follow the Biblical sequence of events as laid out in the scriptures, to discern how much time is left before the end of days. They will see the following: 1) the false peace treaty is signed; 2) the treaty is abrogated three and a half years later; 3) Antichrist enters the Third Temple declares himself god; 4) the devout Jews flee Israel; 5) Antichrist persecutes the saints for forty-two months, which calculates to exactly three and a half years on the Jewish calendar (360 days per year); 6) the end of time. Tracking these events will prevent the saints from walking in darkness regarding the day of the Lord.

Gabriel gave Daniel the calendar to the end of days in a straightforward and clear way, as you can see. Historically the Hebrew scholars recognized this Messianic Clock as revealing the doomsday date in Daniel's prophecies. In the "Targum of the Prophets in the Tractate Megillah" 3a, composed by Rabbi Jonathan ben Uzziel, we read:

> "And the (voice from heaven) came forth and exclaimed, 'who is he that has revealed my secrets to mankind?'

He further sought to reveal by a Targum the inner meaning of the Hagiographa (a portion of scripture which includes Daniel), but a voice from heaven went forth and said, 'Enough! What was the reason? *Because the date of the Messiah was foretold in it*!"

As we have seen, the date of the Messiah is indeed foretold in Daniel, as Rabbi Jonathan ben Uzziel wrote. The ancient Rabbis even knew He would come temporarily the first time, and then rule forever when he returned the second time. The Rosh Hashanah/Yom Kippur prayer book (13th Century Machzor) regarding the coming Messiah has him suffering and reappearing as a new creature.

> "Our righteous Anointed is departed from us: horror has seized us, and we have none to justify us. He has borne the yoke of our iniquities, and our transgression, and is wounded because of our transgression. He bears our sins

on his shoulders, that we may find pardon for our iniquities. We shall be healed by the wounds, at the time that eternal will create the Messiah as a new creature, O bring him up from the circle of the earth. Raise him up from Seir, to assemble us the second time."

In another startling comment in the "Midrash Ruth Rabbah", we find Rabbi Berachya, speaking in the name of Rabbi Levi, declaring:

"He will be with the last deliverer, as with the first (Moses); as the first deliverer revealed himself first to the Israelites and then withdrew, so also will the last deliverer (Messiah) reveal himself to the Israelites and then withdraw for a while." [Midrash Ruth Rabbath 5:6]

As the first deliverer, Moses withdrew for forty years, the second deliverer Messiah, withdrew for forty jubilee years. He will return to deliver His people into the glorious kingdom He promised them. He will defeat the Antichrist and his forces, and set His people free. He will assemble His people when He comes the second time, as Rabbi Jonathan Ben Uzziel foretold.

The book of Zechariah foretells how the Messiah will come to Jerusalem to cleanse the temple 1260 days after its desecration by the Antichrist:

"Then the Lord will go forth and fight against those nations (Armageddon), as He fights in the day of battle. And in that day, His feet will stand on the Mount of Olives, which faces Jerusalem on the east. And the Mount of Olives shall be split in two, from east to west, *making* a very large valley; half of the mountain shall move toward the north and half of it toward the south." [172]

The book of Zechariah identifies the coming Messiah in a startling revelation, when He comes a second time, as Rabbi Jonathan Ben Uzziel predicted. He will be a surprise to the Jews, as Jesus Christ, the One whom they rejected and who was crucified and raised from the dead, appears at the end of time. He was revealed for a short period and withdrew, until the second coming 2000 years (40 jubilee years) later.

He will come back at the end of the last 2,300 days after the erection of the Third Temple. "And he said unto me, unto two thousand and three hundred days; then shall the sanctuary be cleansed." [173] After this temporary period of the Third Temple the Lord Jesus Christ will come to deliver Israel from the Antichrist.

All Israel will see Him whom they pierced, as He comes to deliver them from the Antichrist's attempt to exterminate the Jews from the face of the earth.

> "It shall be in that day *that* I will seek to destroy all the nations that come against Jerusalem. And I will pour on the house of David and on the inhabitants of Jerusalem the Spirit of grace and supplication; *then they will look on Me whom they pierced.* Yes, they will mourn for Him as one mourns for *his* only *son,* and grieve for Him as one grieves for a firstborn. In that day there shall be a great mourning in Jerusalem, like the mourning at Hadad Rimmon in the plain of Megiddo and the land shall mourn, every family by itself: the family of the house of David by itself, and their wives by themselves; the family of the house of Nathan by itself, and their wives by themselves." [174]

The Messianic Clock reveals the preset time for Israel's deliverance, it identifies the Messiah as the one they pierced, and it provides the location where He will appear in Jerusalem, as well as the geological split that His feet will cause on the Mount of Olives. We have detailed accounts, and nothing is left to imagination.

God wants His children to have complete information. He does not want His children to be confused and ignorant of Father's future plans. We have the full prophetic spectrum with startling revelations of events ahead of us. As the Apostle Paul said, we will not be ignorant of that day.

The preset time of 2,300 days constitutes the complete countdown to doomsday, from the rebuilding of the Temple and the daily sacrifice according to the Messianic Clock given to Daniel by Gabriel.

> "And he said to me, "For two thousand three hundred days; then the sanctuary shall be cleansed." [175]

Fundamentally, these will be the last days on earth, which will culminate with the second coming of Christ, "to finish the transgression, and to make an end of sins, and to make reconciliation for iniquity and to bring in everlasting righteousness and to seal up the vision and prophecy, and to anoint the most Holy." [176]

The last 1,260 days are even more definitive: their calculation begins by a very specific event. The Antichrist will break the Land for Peace Treaty. He declares himself as god. This will be a visible sign, observable and recognized by every prophecy watcher of the times and seasons foretold in the Word of God.

> "Then the woman fled into the wilderness, where she has a place prepared by God, that they should feed her there one thousand two hundred and sixty days." [177]

The Jews will flee from Israel. They will be airlifted to safety by a major rescue operation from the coming holocaust. The great tribulation will last 1,260 days before the Messiah rescues the Jews from extermination at the battle of Armageddon.

We have entered the time spectrum when this shabuwa could begin. A shabuwa is a basic time unit on the Messianic Clock. The word shabuwa means 7, or a sabbatical cycle.

The last three and half years will be the time of Jacob's trouble (the great tribulation. This period will be clearly marked by the Antichrist's confirming the peace agreement to establish two states living side by side: Palestine and Israel. This is Gabriel's definitive sign that marks the beginning of the end of time. It is the starting point toward the battle of Armageddon and the end of days.

There will be a short-lived false peace in the Middle East when the Antichrist confirms a seven-year interim peace treaty between Israel and Palestine.

This covenant will allow the Jews to build a Jewish place of worship on Temple Mount, and to restore sacrifices and offerings. This will last for three and a half years before the Antichrist demands that they stop sacrificing. He will then initiate the great tribulation of the saints for three and a half years, or forty-two months. Gabriel specified the period as "a time, times and half a time," exactly three and a half years. [178]

Both the book of Revelation and Daniel vividly portray the Antichrist and his persecution of the saints:

> "He was given a mouth speaking great things and blasphemies and he was given authority to continue for forty two months. And it was granted to him to make war with the saints and to overcome them. And authority was given him over every tribe, tongue and nation." [179]

Forty-two months is exactly three and half years according to the Jewish ancient calculations of thirty days per month.

The visible sign to look for on the time road map to the end of days is the conclusion of the present peace process, when Israel is forced to return to the 1967 border. It is time for you to put on your lifejacket—the Titanic is about to sink into eternal darkness. Following the current road map will lead to Armageddon. The false peace will last for a half shabuwa, or three and a half years.

The second most definitive sign will occur three and a half years after the Rabin Peace Treaty is confirmed, when the head of the New World Order nullifies the treaty. The Jewish worship on Temple Mount will be banned, and the devout Jews will flee to Petra, in Jordan to hide.

THE MESSIANIC CLOCK: TWO THOUSAND YEAR GRACE DISPENSATION FROM THE BAPTISM OF JESUS CHRIST TO CONSUMMATION

Year	Event	Scripture
26 A.D. 81st Jubilee 4,000 years from creation	Jesus Baptized / Heaven Opened and the Spirit Descended Upon Jesus	Luke 3:21 – 22
30 A.D.	Jesus Ministry	Luke 4:14 – 21
	Jesus Triumphant Entry Riding on a Donkey	John 12:9 – 18 Zechariah 9:9
	Jesus Crucifixion	Daniel 9:26 Mark 15:25 – 26
	Jesus Burial	Isaiah 53:9 Matthew 27:57 – 60
	Jesus Resurrection	Matthew 28:5 – 6
	Jesus Ascension	Acts 1:6 – 11
	Pentecost	Acts 2:1 – 4
70 A.D.	Destruction of Jerusalem by Titus	Daniel 9:26 Matthew 24:1 – 2 Luke 21:20 – 22
90 A.D.	Revelation of the Coming Kingdom given to John on the Island of Patmos	Revelations 4:1 –2
135 A.D.	Emperor Hadrian Ploughs Jerusalem	Jeremiah 26:18 Micah 3:12
691 A.D.	The Dome of the Rock / The Abomination of Desolation Erected at the Holy Place on Temple Mount	Daniel 12:11
1026 A.D.	The Whore Church Claims to be the New Israel and Organizes Crusades to take Jerusalem	Revelations 2:9

1536 A.D.	Second Decree to Restore Jerusalem	Daniel 9: 24
1947	United Nations Partition Palestine	Joel 3: 1-2
1967	Israel Captures Temple Mount to Prepare to Build the Third Temple	2 Thessalonians 2:4 Ezekiel 40-48 Revelation 11: 1-8
2012	Beginning of Sorrows	Matthew 24
2026	The End of Days	Daniel 9:24 Matthew 24: 29-57

It should be noted that some scholars calculate the Dispensation of Grace from the birth of the church, which adds a shabuwa to this date. In any case, time as we know it will be no more. Since October 2, 2026 would mark the beginning of the great tribulation in their calculation when "night cometh when no man can work." [180]

CHAPTER FIFTEEN

COUNTDOWN TO ARMAGEDDON UNVEILED

This period before us will constitute a period of global conflicts and rumors of wars, according to the Gabriel Messianic Clock. The world is marching towards World War III. The superpowers are getting ready for war over dwindling natural resources. We are fast approaching nuclear holocaust. We are living in the most dangerous time in history since the end of the Cold War.

> "At the time of the end, the king of the south shall attack him and the king of the north shall come against him like a whirlwind with chariots, horsemen and many ships, and he shall enter the countries, overwhelm them and pass through." [181]

There are two major players, the King of the North with his Shiite Muslim Alliance, and the King of the South with his Sunni Muslim Alliance. Russia is the King of the North, and the head of NATO is the King of the South.

The conflict will be over the Middle East oil resources. The decoy will be the Israeli-Palestinian conflict. Russia will align with Shiite rejectionists, and NATO will support the Sunni position. The Chinese will join in to position themselves for a bigger share of Middle East oil resources. The Middle East oil is the hook that will pull the whole world to the battle of Armageddon. Israel will be the sacrificial lamb.

Jesus, the playwright of the end game, said, "For nation will rise against nation, kingdom against kingdom. And there will be famines, pestilence and earthquakes in various places." [182] It is apparent from scriptures and the signs of the time that we have entered the decade of the end game. The curtains to the final play have been lifted. We know the players—they are identified in the scriptures.

The most momentous play ever written has already begun. We are standing at the threshold of nuclear holocaust and global upheaval. God said it, so you can believe it. That time is short is hard rock absolute truth. You are living in the shadow of an imminent threat. Instead, you need to go and hide under the shadow of the Almighty—immediately! [183]

America as a restraining power is quickly fading, no longer holding back the forces of evil. The Islamic revolution is sweeping across the Middle East, to release Islamic forces of global terrorism and to incite the final Middle East confrontation. Judeo-Christian ethics are being replaced with situational ethics, capitalism with socialism, and nationalism with globalism. Christianity is being replaced with universalism.

The final drama of the ages has begun. The Gabriel Messianic Clock unlocks the secrets and reveals mysteries of this decade and beyond. We are about to see the death of western democracy. All the events predicted for this season are on track to occur.

Israel is about to be forced out of the "West Bank," to the 1967 border, as predicted by the prophet Daniel. Like looking through telescopic zoom lens, we are able to foresee the events of our immediate future.

The prophets' words, written thousands of years ago, are speaking to us today, warning us to prepare to meet our God. The apostle Paul wrote this particularly to our generation:

> "Wherefore gird up the loins of your mind, be sober, and hope to the end for the grace that is to be brought unto you at the revelation of Jesus Christ." [184]

Here are just two of many reasons why expectations should be heightened that we could see in this decade both the seven year peace agreement and the Third Temple in Jerusalem: 1) the replica of the Solomonic Temple is already being designed in preparation to be built in our time; 2) the Rabin peace process is currently being revived. One of the world leaders who is a signer of the peace agreement will in the future declare himself god manifest in the flesh. He will demand that every person on earth take a biochip implant with his number 666.

> "He causes all, both small and great, rich and poor, free and slave, to receive a mark on their right hand or on their foreheads, and that no one may buy or sell except one who has the mark or the name of the beast, or the number of his name. Here is wisdom. Let him who has understanding calculate the number of the beast, for it is the number of a man: his number *is* 666." [185]

The man of sin will be revealed first when he confirms the seven year treaty with Israel and then halfway through the period when he breaks the treaty and moves into the Third Temple in Jerusalem and declares himself god. This is how he is going to be revealed.

THE MESSIANIC CLOCK:
THE PROPHETIC EVENTS 2012 A.D – 2026 A.D.

The Beginning of Sorrows	Luke 21:8-9 Matthew 24:6 II Thessalonians 2:3
The Great Tribulation	Daniel 12:1 Matthew 24:21 Luke 21:12 I Thessalonians 5:9 Revelations 3:10 I Thessalonians 4:15
The Rapture	Matthew 24:2-9 I Thessalonians 3:13 I Thessalonians 4:15 I Thessalonians 4:17
The Apocalypse [Revelations]	I Corinthians 1:7 2 Thessalonians 1:6-7 I Peter 4:13 I Timothy 6:14 II Timothy 4:8 Titus 2:13-14
The Day of The Lord	Joel 2:2 Mark 4:5 I Thessalonians 5:4 II Thessalonians 2:2 II Peter 3:10

GABRIEL MESSIANIC CLOCK:
SECOND DESTRUCTION OF JERUSALEM TO SECOND COMING OF CHRIST

Year	Event	Scripture / Fulfillment
70 A.D.	Destruction of the Second Temple	Matthew 24: 1-2
691 A.D.	The Erection of the Dome of the Rock The Abomination of Desolation Standing at the Holy Place on Temple Mount 1290 years from the Cessation of Sacrifices in 600 B.C.	Daniel 12:11 Matthew 24:15
1536 A.D.	The Second Decree to Restore Jerusalem / The Second Time before the Second Coming of Christ	Daniel 9:25
1967 A.D.	Jerusalem Restored to the Jews in Preparation for the Third Temple	Revelation 11: 1-2
2026 A.D.	70 Shabuwas (70 x 7) from the Second Decree to Restore Jerusalem to Consummation 1536 + 490 years 2026 A.D.	Daniel 9: 24-25

CHAPTER SIXTEEN

THE GABRIEL MESSIANIC CLOCK: UNVEILS THE CELESTRIAL SIGNS TO MARK THE BEGINNING OF SORROWS AND THE END OF TIME (2012 – 2026 A.D.)

The Messianic Clock predicts ominous natural disasters. The Bible links the future horrific ecological disasters to the end of days as signs of His coming.

We will see historically unparalleled super storms, scorching heat, solar storms, killer hailstorms, and climate change, just to mention a few of the divine signs pointing to an end time orchestrated by God. Climate change is not a result of man-made pollution. It is an act of God. It is a sign of things to come. God is orchestrating these natural disasters.

> "Then the fourth angel poured out his bowl on the sun, and power was given to him to scorch men with fire. And men were scorched with great heat, and they blasphemed the name of God who has power over these plagues; and they did not repent and give Him glory." [186]

The earth will experience atmospheric changes. Blazing heat will be a harbinger, one of God's warning signs to mankind to repent before it is too late. God will continue to post more natural disasters as signs, because He desires all men repent and be saved.

God tells us that He will put signs in the sky to try to get our attention, as the Messianic Clock winds down to the end. There shall be signs in the sun and in the moon and in the stars. In this terminal decade, we will very soon see the alignment of these cosmic signs, predicted to happen before the end.

It is not amazing that NASA is predicting some of these signs to happen immediately after September 17, 2012. This is the prophetic time encoded in Daniel as the beginning of the last days, or the beginning of sorrows: the beginning of the last two shabuwas, or seven year cycles, before the termination of time.

"And I will show wonders in the heavens and in the earth: blood and fire and pillars of smoke. The sun shall be turned into darkness, and the moon into blood, before the coming of the great and awesome day of the Lord." [187]

"And there will be signs in the sun, in the moon, and in the stars; and on the earth distress of nations, with perplexity, the sea and the waves roaring." [188]

"I looked when He opened the sixth seal, and behold there was a great earthquake; and the sun became black as sackcloth of hair, and the moon became like blood. And the stars of heaven fell to the earth, as a fig tree drops its late figs when it is shaken by a mighty wind." [189]

"Then the fourth angel sounded: and a third of the sun was struck, a third of the moon, and a third of the stars, so that a third of them were darkened. A third of the day did not shine, and likewise the night." [190]

Even NASA predicts that in this decade, these celestial doomsday signs in the heavens will occur in unusual and peculiar ways: a blackened sun and blood red moons, eclipses and major solar flares, as well as other divine fireworks in the heavens. In other words, many phenomena never seen before are predicted to occur in the next few years. According to Biblical prophecies from thousands of years ago, these signs all herald the coming of the King of Kings.

From the beginning of time, God has preset and prewritten these signs of the times (and their timing) into the structure of the universe. The Bible says, "to everything there is a season, a time for every purpose under heaven." [191]

Modern science is only catching up with Biblical predictions written thousands of years ago. The Messianic Clock forecasts the powers of the heavens being shaken. Joel says, "the earth quakes before them and the heavens tremble, the sun and moon grow dark and the stars diminish their brightness." [192]

ASTRONOMICAL ALIGNMENT ON ROSH HASHANAH

Jesus said, "Great signs shall there be from heaven." [193] When Jesus was born in 4 B.C. there was an astronomical sign in the heavens. John in the book of Revelation describes the sign that led the wise men to go to Jerusalem to worship the King of the Jews. "There appeared a great wonder in heaven: a woman clothed with the sun and the moon under her feet and upon her head a crown of twelve stars... she brought forth a man child who was to rule all nations with a rod of iron: and her child was caught up unto God and to His throne." [194] Jesus is the man-child born, crucified, raised and ascended to the right hand of God in heaven. He is coming back to rule the earth with the rod of iron during the millennium kingdom.

On Rosh Hashanah, September 29, 2011 the same astronomical alignment took place in the constellations. This startling event heralded the first advent of the Messiah. It was a sign of the transition from the Dispensation of the Law to the Dispensation of the Church. This present alignment is pointing to the impending transition to the age of the Kingdom. God reveals the times and seasons through the signs in the heavens. "God said, let there be light in the firmament of the heaven to divide the day from night and let them be for signs and for seasons and for days and years." [195] The Bible tells us "the heavens declare the Glory of God" [196] He has written the redemption story in the constellations.

God says He will shake the powers of the heavens in these last days. The earth will complete in this decade a processional cycle that takes 26,000 years. For the first time, the earth will cross the threshold of the Milky Way's equator, which intercepts the black hole at the center of our galaxy.

This could be a possible cause of the earth quaking and the heavens trembling as foretold in scripture. Some scientists believe this is the graveyard of stars, and where new stars are born.

The effects of planetary alignment in this decade could cause monumental impact on this planet that could threaten human survival. We can turn to the Bible to give us a preview of what is going to happen in this decade, predicted thousands of years ago: "The earth will quake and the heavens will tremble."[197] This event will take place as predicted by the sacred Hebrew literature to signal the end of days. It does not mark the end; it just marks the beginning of the end.

The year 2012 is critical as it initiates the last two sabbatical cycles. These two shabuwas represent a period in the last days in which there will be an increase in natural disasters and ecological upheavals. This date is a tipping point, a change of seasons.

During this sabbatical seven-year cycle, there will be one set of blood red moons on the Feasts of the Lord, in one Jewish year. It is the only set in this century—a major sign of the times.[198]

1. Passover April 15, 2014
2. Sukkoth October 8, 2014
3. Passover April 4, 2015
4. Sukkoth September 28, 2015

These cosmic signs of blood red moons are traditionally regarded as signaling wars and rumors of wars. Jesus said, "There will be signs in the sun, moon and stars."[199] These will signal the approaching cataclysmic events.

> "And you will hear of wars and rumors of wars. See that you are not troubled; for all *these things* must come to pass, but the end is not yet. For nation will rise against nation, and kingdom against kingdom. And there will be famines, pestilences and earthquakes in various places. All these *are* the beginning of sorrows." [200]

SIGNS IN THE HEAVENS DURING THE
SIXTY-NINTH AND SEVENTIETH WEEK OF DANIEL

Year	Event	Scripture
This Decade 69th Week of Daniel	Planetary Alignment Powers of the Heavens Shaken	Joel 2:10
November 13-14, 2013	The Sun Darkened Solar Eclipse	Luke 21:25
April 15, 2014	Red Blood Moon on Passover	Joel 3:31
October 8, 1014	Red Blood Moon on Sukkot	Joel 3:31
April 4, 2015	Red Blood Moon on Passover	Joel 3:31
September 28, 2015	Red Blood Moon Shaken	Joel 3:31
September 29, 2019	The 70th week of Daniel from the Second Decree to Restore Jerusalem	Daniel 9:24
October 2, 2026 A.D.	The End of the 70th Week of Daniel End of Time	Daniel 12:12

CHAPTER SEVENTEEN

THE MESSIANIC CLOCK: THE GLORY OF GOD RETURNS TO TEMPLE MOUNT INTO THE THIRD TEMPLE

As I am writing this book, devout Jews are planning to build an exact replica of the Solomonic Temple, which I believe is the Temple that will be moved to Temple Mount. The current observers of the present tension in the region think it will be impossible to move the Jewish Temple to Temple Mount. God has a set time for the Third Temple to be erected on Mount Moriah, and that time is near. There is not a power on earth that can stop it.

The Antichrist will take credit for this monumental achievement. He will immediately claim to be the long awaited Messiah. At the beginning, it will be the Antichrist's ticket to fame and world domination. At the same time, it will be a source of tension in the Muslim world, and it will force him to betray the Jews three and a half years later.

The Antichrist will sign a seven year Middle East Peace Treaty, which officially marks the last seven years before the battle of Armageddon. This is a watermark event, a momentous moment in history.

The prophet Ezekiel saw the Glory of God fill the Third Temple. We know that Ezekiel's Temple is not the Millennium Temple because a wall is built to separate it from the profane thing, the Dome of the Rock.

> "He measured it by the four sides: it had a wall round about, five hundred reeds long, and five hundred broad, to make a separation between the sanctuary and the profane place." [201]

As I shared before, John in the book of Revelation gives us further precise location of the profane thing, the Dome of the Rock, the Abomination of Desolation spoken of by the prophet Daniel. It was erected at the court of the Gentiles.

"And there was given me a reed like unto a rod: and the angel stood, saying, Rise, and measure the temple of God, and the altar, and them that worship therein. But the court which is without the temple leave out, and measure it not; for it is given unto the Gentiles: and the holy city shall they tread under foot forty and two months." [202]

Ezekiel describes in great detail the coming glory that will fill the Third Temple. The Lord will come into the Third Temple in great Glory.

"And, behold, the glory of the God of Israel came from the way of the east: and his voice was like a noise of many waters: and the earth shined with his glory." [203]

"And the glory of the LORD came into the house by the way of the gate whose prospect is toward the east. So the spirit took me up, and brought me into the inner court; and, behold, the glory of the LORD filled the house.
And I heard him speaking unto me out of the house; and the man stood by me. And he said unto me, Son of man, the place of my throne, and the place of the soles of my feet, where I will dwell in the midst of the children of Israel for ever, and my holy name, shall the house of Israel no more defile, neither they, nor their kings, by their whoredom, nor by the carcasses of their kings in their high places." [204]

The Antichrist will defile the Third Temple. He will sit in the Third Temple acting like god until the triumphant return of Christ when he will be destroyed.

"And who opposes and exalts himself above all that is called God or that is worshiped, so that he sits as God in the temple of God, showing himself that he is God And then the lawless one will be revealed, whom the Lord will consume with the breath of His mouth and destroy with the brightness of His coming." [205]

The final battle on earth will be over Jerusalem and Temple Mount. God put His name on Temple Mount forever. God says, this is the place of my Throne and the place of the soles of my feet where I dwell in the midst of the children of Israel forever.

The devil wants to take the place of God and claim to be god. God has appointed Jesus Ruler of the universe. The devil has appointed Antichrist to rule the universe from Jerusalem in opposition to God's plan.

The Daniel Messianic Clock is anchored on Temple Mount. It is the epicenter of the cosmic conflict as a place of His millennium throne on earth. The forces of evil will fight to occupy the place where god wrote His name in the topography, the tetragrammaton YHWH. The Midrash says this about Temple Mount.

"The Holy One blessed by He to have an abode below just as He has one above. When Israel stood before Him at Mount Sinai He told them. There is only one reason I delivered you out of Egypt in order for you to erect for me a tabernacle so that my presence will dwell among you."

The terminal war will be fought over Temple Mount. Daniel gave us a sequence of events that are going to happen in the end of days. Jerusalem was restored twice to the Jews. The first return from Babylon they built the Second Temple and the second return from the Diaspora they will build the Third Temple. The Third Temple in Jerusalem on Temple Mount will trigger the battle of Armageddon.

The Rabbinic tradition maintains that the Temple treasures are still under the Temple Mount. In 1967 the Jews took control of Temple Mount after 1,900 years to set a stage for the final conflict over its future. Daniel predicts that the Antichrist will desecrate the Third Temple. He will set up the image of the beast in the Temple. The book of Revelation describes what it is:

> "And he deceives those who dwell on the earth by those signs which he was granted to do in the sight of the beast, telling those who dwell on the earth to make an image to the beast who was wounded by the sword and lived. He was granted power to give breath to the image of the beast, that the image of the beast should both speak and cause as many as would not worship the image of the beast to be killed." [206]

Daniel gives us the timetable to when these events will take place. John tells us what events will take place. It is clearly identified on the Messianic Clock that during the middle of the last seven-year sabbatical cycle initiated by the Peace Treaty in Israel the Antichrist will set up His image in the Third Temple.

The focus of world events will increasingly become fixed on Jerusalem. It will dominate world news. Titus destroyed it in 70 A.D. For over 86 times it experienced wars. Jerusalem has been a source of conflict for 4,000 years. In 1980 the Jews made Jerusalem their national capital.

The Arabs want East Jerusalem or the Biblical Jerusalem to be the capital of the Palestinian state. The Holy One of Israel put His name on Temple Mount forever. They want to replace him with Allah the god of Islam. They want the name of Allah to be there forever and not the Holy One of Israel. He will intervene to deliver Jerusalem when the armies of the Gentiles surround it.

> "But when you see Jerusalem surrounded by armies, then know that its desolation is near. Then let those who are in Judea flee to the mountains, let those who are in the midst of her depart, and let not those who are in the country enter her.

For these are the days of vengeance, that all things which are written may be fulfilled. But woe to those who are pregnant and to those who are nursing babies in those days! For there will be great distress in the land and wrath upon this people. And they will fall by the edge of the sword, and be led away captive into all nations.

And Jerusalem will be trampled by Gentiles until the times of the Gentiles are fulfilled. And there will be signs in the sun, in the moon, and in the stars; and on the earth distress of nations, with perplexity, the sea and the waves roaring; men's hearts failing them from fear and the expectation of those things which are coming on the earth, for the powers of the heavens will be shaken. Then they will see the Son of Man coming in a cloud with power and great glory." [207]

As the armies of the world surround Jerusalem to take it back from the Jews and to kill every Jew in the final holocaust, the Lord Jesus will rend the heavens open and come down with the host of heaven to deliver Israel and destroy the greatest army ever assembled on earth. The blood will run up to the horses bridle. It will cover 200 miles, a distance from Bozrah to Megiddo.

"Who *is* this who comes from Edom, With dyed garments from Bozrah, This *One who is* glorious in His apparel, Traveling in the greatness of His strength? I who speak in righteousness, mighty to save. Why *is* Your apparel red, and Your garments like one who treads in the winepress? I have trodden the winepress alone, and from the peoples no one *was* with Me. For I have trodden them in My anger, and trampled them in My fury; Their blood is sprinkled upon My garments, and I have stained all My robes. For the day of vengeance *is* in My heart, and the year of my redeemed has come." [208]

The Lord Jesus and the Holy Angels will descend from heaven and fight against the Antichrist and his forces in the battle of Armageddon.

"Now I saw heaven opened, and behold, a white horse. And He who sat on him *was* called Faithful and True, and in righteousness He judges and makes war. His eyes *were* like a flame of fire, and on His head *were* many crowns. He had a name written that no one knew except Himself. He *was* clothed with a robe dipped in blood, and His name is called The Word of God.

And the armies in heaven, clothed in fine linen, white and clean followed Him on white horses. Now out of His mouth goes a sharp sword, that with it He should strike the nations. And He Himself will rule them with a rod of iron.

He Himself treads the winepress of the fierceness and wrath of Almighty God. And He has on *His* robe and on His thigh a name written: KING OF KINGS AND LORD OF LORDS.

Then I saw an angel standing in the sun; and he cried with a loud voice, saying to all the birds that fly in the midst of heaven, Come and gather together for the supper of the great God that you may eat the flesh of kings, the flesh of captains, the flesh of mighty men, the flesh of horses and of those who sit on them, and the flesh of all *people,* free and slave, both small and great.

And I saw the beast, the kings of the earth, and their armies, gathered together to make war against Him who sat on the horse and against His army.

Then the beast was captured, and with him the false prophet who worked signs in his presence, by which he deceived those who received the mark of the beast and those who worshiped his image. These two were cast alive into the lake of fire burning with brimstone.

 And the rest were killed with the sword which proceeded from the mouth of Him who sat on the horse. And all the birds were filled with their flesh." [209]

This will bring the long history of Jerusalem and the Holy Land wars, conquests and destruction to an end after 4,000 years. In 2026 B.C. Melchizedek King of Salem, a High Priest without beginning or end ruled the city. In 1026 B.C. Solomon built the Temple and the Glory of God filled it. In 30 A.D. Jesus Christ was crucified, rose again and ascended to Heaven from Jerusalem. He will descend from heaven to defend His beloved city in the end of time in our generation and to cleanse the Temple.

THE MESSIANIC CLOCK
JERUSALEM EPICENTER/TEMPLE MOUNT GROUND ZERO
FOUR THOUSAND YEAR HISTORY

Year	Event	Scripture
2026 B.C.	Melchizedek Rules Salem	Genesis 14: 18-20 Hebrews 6:20, 7:22
1026 B.C.	The Glory Filled Solomon's Temple	2 Chronicles 5:13-14
600 B.C.	Nebuchadnezzar Destroys Solomon's Temple	2 Kings 24-25 2 Chronicles 36
515 B.C.	The Second Temple	Haggai 2: 18-19
332 B.C.	Greek Conquest of the Holy Land	Daniel 8: 21-23
168 A.D.	Antiochus Epiphanies Defiles the Second Temple	Daniel 8:9, 11: 21-25
63 A.D.	Roman Conquest of the Holy Land	John 19:15
30 A.D.	Jesus Christ Crucified in Jerusalem and Rose again from the Dead	Matthew 27-28 Luke 23-24
691 A.D.	The Dome of the Rock Built. Abomination of Desolation	Daniel 12:11 Matthew 24:15
1536 A.D.	Suleiman the Magnificent makes the Second Decree to Restore Jerusalem	Daniel 9: 25-26 Daniel 9:24
1917 A.D.	Palestine Liberated from the Ottoman Empire	Isaiah 31:5
1967 A.D.	Jerusalem Restored to the Jews in the Six Day War	Joel 3:1-3 Zechariah 12:5-6
1980 A.D.	Jerusalem Declared the Jewish Capital	2 Chronicles 6:6, 7:16
2012-2026 A.D.	End of Time Events	Zechariah 12: 2-5

CHAPTER EIGHTEEN

THE DANIEL MESSIANIC CLOCK: ALIGNMENT WITH THE MOSES TORAH VERSES/YEAR CODE PROPHECY

Moses was given the Torah by God. Concealed in the Torah is what I call the Moses code, an amazing correspondence of the Torah verse and the Jewish year prediction. The verse chronicles the future events, preset to happen in that Jewish year.

The Daniel Messianic Clock concealed in the message from God, delivered by the angel Gabriel, correlates with perfect precision with the sequence of events and chronology, preset in the song of Moses. The mathematical design of the Bible encodes mysteries regarding future events.

The numerical value of the words in the Bible reveals divine precision concerning future events. As an example, there are seven words in the first verse of the (Hebrew) Bible. The number seven represents divine perfection. There are three nouns in the first verse: God, heaven, and earth. The numerical value of these three nouns is 777.

The numerical value code of the tetragrammaton YHWH is 26. The first day of creation was Rosh Hashanah 4026 B.C.. The end of time will be Rosh Hashanah 2026 A.D. He is the Author and Finisher. The original acreage of the Temple Mount was 26. The tetragrammaton is written on the topography of Temple Mount.

In the Hebrew Bible text, verse 26 reveals God's plan for the future:

> "Then God said, 'Let us make mankind in our image, in our likeness, so that they may rule over the fish in the sea and the birds in the sky, over the livestock and all the wild animals, and over all the creatures that move along the ground." [210]

On the last day of creation, the sixth day, God made man in His own image, to rule and to reign on earth. Again at the end of the last day from creation, the sixth millennium, God will translate man into His image in a twinkling of an eye at the rapture.

> "Beloved, now we are children of God; and it has not yet been revealed what we shall be, but we know that when He is revealed, we shall be like Him, for we shall see Him as He is." [211]

He will give the saints dominion on the earth to rule again for a thousand years. What man lost through the fall will be restored: full authority and dominion on the earth. The blood of Jesus purchased man from the consequences of sin.

> "And they sang a new song, saying, 'You are worthy to take the scroll, and to open its seals; for You were slain, and have redeemed us to God by Your blood out of every tribe and tongue and people and nation, and have made us kings and priests to our God; and we shall reign on the earth." [212]

God encoded the blessed hope in the very beginning of time and throughout the scriptures Christ is featured as the hope of the ages. The hour is quickly approaching when the saints will be transformed into His likeness and will receive dominion on this earth.

> "Then the kingdom and dominion, and the greatness of the kingdoms under the whole heaven, shall be given to the people, the saints of the Most High. His kingdom *is* an everlasting kingdom, and all dominions shall serve and obey Him." [213]

Moses was not only shown the Holy Land from Mt. Pisgah, but he was projected down the corridor of time to the end of days. He wrote about the final restoration of Israel back to their ancient land, before the advent of the Millennium Kingdom.

The verse-year prophetic correlation points to the Jewish year 5708 (Julian year 1948 A.D.) as the beginning of that restoration. Israel's rebirth as a nation is a key stepping stone that leads eventually but certainly to the advent of the Messiah.

> "That the Lord your God will bring you back from captivity, and have compassion on you, and gather you again from all the nations where the Lord your God has scattered you." [214]

The Ramban Rabbi Moses ben Nachman, an outstanding sage also called Nachmanides, is quoted as saying, "I maintain that all history is hinted at in the song of Moses." Needless to say, the whole history of Israel is encrypted in the song of Moses, with amazing details: times of the Gentiles, the Diaspora, the issue of land for peace, the battle of Armageddon and the Millennium kingdom.

The Song of Moses and the Jewish year correlates until the end of day's events and the preset time when each depicted event will take place. The Gabriel Messianic Clock is in perfect harmony with the sequence of events in the song of Moses.

The period concealed in the song of Moses converges with the timeline in Daniel with perfect precision. Daniel is told to seal the message until the end of days, when God will reveal it to the wise. Scripture will interpret scripture, here a little and there a little, until the puzzle of the ages is completed and the picture revealed.

The prophetic backdrop provides the setting for our Biblical understanding of the endtime events before us in this generation. The future events have been chronicled in detail for us to know the urgency of this hour.

According to the Moses code and Messianic Clock in Daniel, this generation will come suddenly and unexpectedly to terminal catastrophe. The song of Moses gives us the precise timing, while the Daniel Messianic clock reveals that this event will take place after the second exile and second decree to restore Jerusalem. God set the timetable in the book of Daniel.

The Jewish year/verse prophecy pinpoints the year 5773 (Julian year 2012) as the beginning of the end of days. It happens to be the beginning of the 69th "week" of Daniel after Suleiman made the decree to restore Jerusalem. Also, from the song of Moses:

> "But Jeshurun grew fat and kicked; you grew fat, you grew thick, you are obese! Then he forsook God who made him and scornfully esteemed the Rock of his salvation." [215]

Jeshurun (God's beloved people) grew fat and sleek and forsook their God as their shield and protector. They turn to the Gentile superpowers to give them security guarantees in exchange for signing a peace treaty with the Palestinians, rather than turning to God for their protection and security. They put their future into the hands of the multinational forces of the New World Order, instead of trusting God, who brought them back as a nation after an absence of 1900 years.

They will forsake God who made them and scorn the Rock of their salvation. They make Him jealous with strange gods. Daniel describes these strange gods predicted in the Song of Moses as the Antichrist and his military forces. He will act as their false protector and god until the battle of Armageddon.

> "He shall regard neither the God of his fathers nor the desire of women, nor regard any god; for he shall exalt himself above *them* all. But in their place he shall honor a god of fortresses; and a god which his fathers did not know, he shall honor with gold and silver, with precious stones and pleasant things." [216]

Israel will disregard the God of Abraham, Isaac and Jacob and put their trust in Antichrist's space-based weapons of mass destruction, and in their treaty with him. This treaty constitutes a pact with the devil himself. The Antichrist is the devil incarnate (in human form). The political leadership in Israel in this decade will reject God as their shield and protector, and choose instead the Antichrist. This is God's warning to them:

> "Therefore hear the word of the Lord, you scornful men, who rule this people who are in Jerusalem, because you have said, 'We have made a covenant with death, and with Sheol we are in agreement. When the overflowing scourge passes through, it will not come to us, for we have made lies our refuge, and under falsehood we have hidden ourselves." [217]

In the Messianic Clock, the prophet Isaiah describes the political agreement enshrined in the Israeli-Palestinian peace agreement as a treaty with death and hell. This agreement constitutes the forsaking of God, predicted in Moses' song. The Antichrist will gain access to the Temple, and he will sit in it, declaring himself god. He will break his treaty with Israel and begin the final holocaust for three and a half years.

> "Then he shall confirm a covenant with many for one week; but in the middle of the week he shall bring an end to sacrifice and offering. And on the wing of abominations shall be one who makes desolate, even until the consummation, which is determined, is poured out on the desolate." [218]

MYSTERY BABYLON: THE REVIVED ROMAN EMPIRE

Ancient Babylon is a type and shadow of the Antichrist kingdom. It is a blueprint of the New World Order in the end of days. The Antichrist is called the King of Babylon. The time of his judgment is superimposed in the Ancient Babylonian preset time.

> "And it shall come to pass, when seventy years are accomplished, that I will punish the king of Babylon, and that nation, says the LORD, for their iniquity, and the land of the Chaldeans, and will make it perpetual desolations." [219]

The judgment of Babylon took place exactly seventy years from the time it subjected Israel. The set pattern for mystery Babylon's preset time of destruction from its inception in 1957 when the Treaty of Rome was signed to revive the ancient Roman Empire is at the end of seventy years. John was shown the fall of the New World Order.

> "And he cried mightily with a loud voice, saying, 'Babylon the great is fallen, is fallen, and has become a dwelling place of demons, a prison for every foul spirit, and a cage for every unclean and hated bird!" [220]

The revived Roman Empire will establish the New World Order, one world government headed by the Antichrist. He will be the last world ruler. He will claim to be god manifest in the flesh. The time template for the fall of mystery Babylon (New World Order) is "when seventy years are accomplished" from the resurrection of the Roman Empire.

The date according to Jewish reckoning corresponds exactly with the end of the Daniel Messianic Clock for the end of time. The divine timeline is consistent throughout the scriptures. The pattern synchronizes with perfect precision with Moses' verse/year/prophecy correlation. It harmonizes with the end of six thousand years from creation, the Genesis and Noahic Time Template.

NUMERICAL VALUE OF THE JEWISH YEAR 5788

The Messianic Clock is definitive and gives a consistent termination date throughout the scriptures. The Moses year/verse/prophecy aligns with the Messianic Clock delivered to Daniel by Gabriel. The Jewish year 5788 is the end of history, as we have known it. The year/verse/prophecy confirms it. The numerical value of the year attests to it.

The number five is grace: God's grace for His children. He will deliver them from the Antichrist. It is the year of the manifestation of His redeeming grace and kingdom. The number seven is divine perfection or completion. It is the year of the completion of His purpose for creation. It is a completion of six thousand years of mankind's labor.

The Bible tells us that one day to God is like one thousand years, and a thousand years as a day. The final (seventh) thousand year will be the Sabbath rest for the people of God.

The number eight represents new beginning. It is also the number for Jesus as the author of a new beginning. Double eights (88) point to the beginning of the millennium kingdom, and to the new heaven and the new earth after the millennium kingdom.

MESSIANIC CLOCK: TORAH VERSES/YEAR CORRELATION

Roman Year	Jewish Year	Bible Verse	Prediction	Confirmation or Signs of the Time
1948	5708	5708	"That the Lord your God will bring you back from captivity, and have compassion on you, and gather you again from all the nations where the Lord your God has scattered you." Deuteronomy 30:3	The rebirth of Israel
2012	5773	5773	"But Jeshurun grew fat and kicked; You grew fat, you grew thick, You are obese! Then he forsook God *who* made him, and scornfully esteemed the Rock of his salvation." Deuteronomy 32:15	69th week of Daniel Beginning of sorrows
2013	5774	5774	"They provoked Him to jealousy with foreign *gods;* With abominations they provoked Him to anger." Deuteronomy 32:16	Time window opens up, Israel receives multinational security guarantees in exchange for signing the treaty
2014	5775	5775	"They sacrificed to demons, not to God, to gods they did not know, To new gods, new arrivals That your fathers did not fear." Deuteronomy 32:17	Trust in False Security

2015	5776	5776	Of the Rock who begot you, you are unmindful, and have forgotten the God who fathered you. Deuteronomy 32:18	Rejection of God of Abraham, Isaac and Jacob
2016	5777	5777	"And when the LORD saw it, He spurned them, because of the provocation of His sons and His daughters." Deuteronomy 32:19	God lifts his Protective Hand
2017	5778	5778	And He said: 'I will hide My face from them, I will see what their end will be, for they are a perverse generation, children in whom is no faith." Deuteronomy 32:20	God Hides His Face from Israel
2018	5779	5779	They have provoked Me to jealousy by what is not God; They have moved Me to anger by their foolish idols but I will provoke them to jealousy by those who are not a nation; I will move them to anger by a foolish nation." Deuteronomy 32:21	God is Angry Those Who Are Not a People (Nation) Palestinians
2019	5780	5780	For a fire is kindled in My anger, and shall burn to the lowest hell; It shall consume the earth with her increase, and set on fire the foundations of the mountains." Deuteronomy 32:22	A fire will be kindled by God

MESSIANIC CLOCK: TORAH VERSE/YEAR CORRELATION
(2020-2027 A.D.)

2020	5781	5781	'I will heap disasters on them; I will spend My arrows on them." Deuteronomy 32:23	Divine Judgment
2021	5782	5782	"They shall be wasted with hunger, devoured by pestilence and bitter destruction; I will also send against them the teeth of beasts, with the poison of serpents of the dust." Deuteronomy 32:24	The wrath of God is Poured Out
2022	5783	5783	"The sword shall destroy outside; There shall be terror within for the young man and virgin, the nursing child with the man of gray hairs." Deuteronomy 32:25	War and Blood Shed
2023	5784	5784	I would have said, "I will dash them in pieces, I will make the memory of them to cease from among men," Deuteronomy 32:26	Great Peril and Distress
2024	5785	5785	Had I not feared the wrath of the enemy, lest their adversaries should misunderstand, lest they should say, "Our hand is high; And it is not the Lord who has done all this." Deuteronomy 32:27	God Intervenes

2025	5786	5786	"For they are a nation void of counsel, nor is there any understanding in them." Deuteronomy 32:28	Israel in its Apostate State
2026	5787	5787	"Oh, that they were wise, that they understood this, that they would consider their latter end!" Deuteronomy 32:29	The Lord Redeems Israel and Restores them to Himself
2026	October 2 Rosh Hashanah 2026 A.D.	5788	"How could one chase a thousand, and two put ten thousand to flight, unless their Rock had sold them, and the LORD had surrendered them? Deuteronomy 32:30 For their rock is not like our Rock, even our enemies themselves being judges." Deuteronomy 32:31	

* Jesus said the Divine calendar of the end events has been shortened for the sake of the elect. There is acceleration towards the end to make it much, much sooner for the sake of the elect.

CHAPTER NINETEEN

MESSIANIC CODE: IN THE YEAR 2026 A.D. JULIAN CALENDAR ENCODED THE CONSUMMATION OF HISTORY

Our God is a God of mathematical precision. There is a paradigm preset by God from creation. This is particularly true when it comes to the Biblical timeline to consummation. The days of Lot occurred in 2026 B.C., when God destroyed Sodom and Gomorrah, "as it was in the days of Lot." [221] In 2026 A.D. the consummation of history will come.

The year 2026 is a combination of two Biblical numbers: 20 and 26. The number 20 represents the completion of probation and chastisement:

1. Jacob waited 20 years to get his wives. [222]
2. Israel waited 20 years for deliverance from Jabin's oppression. [223]
3. The Ark of Covenant stayed 20 years at Kirjath Jearim, before it was restored. [224]

The number 26, as we have discussed before, is the numerical value of the tetragammaton, the four letters of YHWH. The year 2026 A.D. is the end of man's chastisement. God will restore His Tabernacle and dwell with man again.

In the year 26 A.D., the Messiah was revealed immediately after John baptized Him.

> "When He had been baptized, Jesus came up immediately from the water; and behold, the heavens were opened to Him, and He saw the Spirit of God descending like a dove and alighting upon Him. And suddenly a voice came from heaven, saying, 'This is My beloved Son, in whom I am well pleased." [225]

Exactly after two days of a thousand years each He will revive us on the third day. He will raise us up in the year 2026 A.D. precisely 2,000 years after 26 A.D. The Dispensation of Grace will be over, and the age of the Kingdom will begin.

> "Come, and let us return to the LORD; For He has torn, but He will heal us; He has stricken, but He will bind us up. After *two days* He will revive us; On the third day He will raise us up, that we may live in His sight. Let us know, let us pursue the knowledge of the LORD. His going forth is established as the morning; He will come to us like the rain, like the latter *and* former rain to the earth." [226]

God will restore the kingdom to Israel after two days or 2,000 years from the time of Jesus First Advent when He was rejected. Israel was scattered among the nations as wandering Jews until 1948. They are back in the land to fulfill all the prophecies regarding the last days before the Advent of the Messianic Kingdom after two days.

CHAPTER TWENTY

THE MESSIANIC CLOCK: THE PRESERVATION OF THE SAINTS FROM THE GREAT TRIBULATION

The scriptures are clear that the overcomers, holy and pure, are kept away from the great tribulation. They will be hidden away. They will be separated and put under heaven's shield. God will put a seal on them unto preservation. No weapon formed against them will prosper. For those who keep His commandments, God will keep them away from the tribulation.

> "Because you have kept My command to persevere, I also will keep you from the hour of trial which shall come upon the whole world, to test those who dwell on the earth." [227]

The saints that are walking in holiness are exempt from the great tribulation. They are kept away. God will separate them as He did in Egypt. Goshen was kept away from the judgment of God. "For God did not appoint us to wrath, but to obtain salvation through our Lord Jesus Christ." [228]

God is in control of the great tribulation. The Antichrist is God's Antichrist. He is God's rod of indignation, cleansing a compromised church in order to make her without spot or wrinkle, ready to meet the Lord in the air.

> "And some of those of understanding shall fall, *to refine them, purify them and make them white,* until the time of the end: because it is still for the appointed time." [229]

The saints that have made themselves ready and are walking in obedience to the Lord He promised to keep them away from tribulation. They are not the objects of God's chastening.

"For whom the LORD loves He chastens, and scourges every son whom He receives. If you endure chastening, God deals with you as with sons; for what son is there whom a father does not chasten? But if you are without chastening, of which all have become partakers, then you are illegitimate and not sons. Now no chastening seems to be joyful for the present, but painful; nevertheless, afterward it yields the peaceable fruit of righteousness to those who have been trained by it." [230]

The question is, where are the overcomers kept? The Pre-Tribulation proponents believe they will be raptured, snatched away in the air with the Lord. Proponents of Post-Tribulation say that as it was in the days of Noah, they will be preserved on the earth.

They point to the protected children of Israel in Goshen during God's judgment in Egypt. God protected the church at Petra during the destruction of Jerusalem by Titus in 70 A.D. The early Church was kept away during that terrible holocaust. God is in control of the great tribulation.

The Antichrist is God's instrument to cleanse God's compromised children to prepare them to meet the Lord through the cleansing of the fire of persecution. He wants none of His chosen to be left behind because they are spotted and winkled. All of God's children will be gathered unto Him, none will be lost. "He that begun a good work in them will finish it." [231]

The Pre-Tribulationists build their strongest argument about the removal of saints from the earth to meet the Lord in the air based on this passage:

"I tell you, in that night there will be two men in one bed: the one will be taken and the other will be left. Two women will be grinding together: the one will be taken and the other left. Two men will be in the field: the one will be taken and the other left. And they answered and said to Him, Where Lord? So He said to them, *Wherever the carcass is, there the eagles* (or vultures) *will be gathered together."* [232]

This passage contains the crux of the disagreement, since the disciples asked Jesus where those who disappeared are taken. We do not have to guess or wonder, He gave a clear answer, "For wherever the carcass is, there will the vultures be gathered together." [233] He did not say, to meet the Lord in the air.

The book of Revelation tells us where the carcass is and where the vultures will be gathered in the last days, at the Great Supper of God:

"And the armies which were in heaven followed him upon white horses, clothed in fine linen, white and clean. And out of his mouth goes a sharp sword, that with it he should smite the nations: and he shall rule them with a rod of iron: and he treads the winepress of the fierceness and wrath of Almighty God. And he hath on his vesture and on his thigh a name written, KING OF KINGS, AND LORD OF LORDS.

Then I saw an angel standing in the sun; and he cried with a loud voice, saying to all the birds that fly in the midst of heaven, "Come and gather together for the supper of the great God, that you may eat the flesh of kings, the flesh of captains, the flesh of mighty men, the flesh of horses and of those who sit on them, and the flesh of all people, free and slave, both small and great. And I saw the beast, and the kings of the earth, and their armies, gathered together to make war against him that sat on the horse, and against his army.

And the beast was taken, and with him the false prophet that wrought miracles before him, with which he deceived them that had received the mark of the beast, and them that worshipped his image. These both were cast alive into a lake of fire burning with brimstone. And the remnant were slain with the sword of him that sat upon the horse, which sword proceeded out of his mouth: and all the fowls were filled with their flesh." [234]

The scripture interprets scripture. John tells us where the carcass is and the vultures will be gathered. The reason it is important to notice is because they are taken to a place of dead bodies where vultures are gathered, not to meet the Lord in the air. There will be no carcass when the saints meet the Lord in the air. Heaven is not a place of dead bodies and vultures gathering to consume the dead.

The prophet Ezekiel pinpoints the place they are taken and gathered at the Great Supper of the Lord, "Where the carcass is, there also the vultures are gathered." [235]

"And as for you, son of man, thus says the Lord GOD, Speak to every sort of bird and to every beast of the field: Assemble yourselves and come; Gather together from all sides to My sacrificial meal which I am sacrificing for you, a great sacrificial meal on the mountains of Israel, That you may eat flesh and drink blood.

Ye shall eat the flesh of the mighty, and drink the blood of the princes of the earth, of rams, of lambs, and of goats, of bullocks, all of them fatlings of Bashan. And ye shall eat fat till ye be full, and drink blood till ye be drunken, of my sacrifice which I have sacrificed for you. Thus ye shall be filled at my table with horses and chariots, with mighty men, and with all men of war, says the Lord GOD." [236]

They will be taken to the valley of Jehoshaphat where they will gather for God's judgment. The Lord Jesus will destroy them by a sharp sword out of His mouth. God says "I will also gather all nations and bring them, "one will be taken and the other left" [237] to the valley of Jehoshaphat to enter into judgment there.

> "I will also gather all nations and bring them down to the Valley of Jehoshaphat; and I will enter into judgment with them there on account of My people, My heritage Israel, whom they have scattered among the nations; they have also divided up My land." [238]

The other problematic passage regarding Pre-Tribulation rapture is when Jesus speaks about the final sequence of events at the end of days, regarding who is going to disappear first, or be taken away first:

> "Another parable put he forth unto them, saying, The kingdom of heaven is likened unto a man which sowed good seed in his field: But while men slept, his enemy came and sowed tares among the wheat, and went his way. But when the blade was sprung up, and brought forth fruit, then appeared the tares also. So the servants of the householder came and said unto him, Sir, didst not thou sow good seed in thy field? from whence then hath it tares? He said unto them, An enemy hath done this.
> The servants said unto him, Wilt thou then that we go and gather them up? But he said, Nay; lest while ye gather up the tares, ye root up also the wheat with them.
> Let both grow together until the harvest: and in the time of harvest I will say to the reapers, *Gather ye together first the tares, and bind them in bundles to burn them*: but gather the wheat into my barn. The field is the world; the good seed are the children of the kingdom; but the tares are the children of the wicked one; The enemy that sowed them is the devil; the harvest is the end of the world; and the reapers are the angels. As therefore the tares are

gathered and burned in the fire; so shall it be in the end of this world.

The Son of man shall send forth his angels, and they shall gather out of his kingdom all things that offend, and them which do iniquity." [239]

Here again the Post-Tribulation proponents points out that Jesus clearly says, "First gather up the tares and bind them in bundles to burn them." He did not say, "Send the angels to gather the wheat (the saints) first, but rather the tares", [240] (sons of the evil one). This conflicts with the popular (Pre-Tribulation) belief.

The fact that Jesus Himself said it makes it clear that the first disappearance when one is taken and one is left behind, is of the wicked, before the saints are gathered unto Him in the air. The one taken first will be taken to the place of the carcasses, where the vultures are gathered.

"May sinners be consumed from the earth, and the wicked be no more. Bless the LORD, O my soul! Praise the LORD!" [241]

Both Pre-Tribulation and Post-Tribulation proponents agree that the overcomers will be kept away "from the hour of testing, that hour which is about to come upon the whole world to test those who dwell upon the earth." [242] Since it is clear that the saints are going to be preserved and kept away from the hour of testing, there is no controversy about it.

The exciting issue is not where they kept, but rather that they are kept. That is the good news. Rather than speak where the Bible is silent, it is best to be silent where the Bible is silent. The geography of where they are kept is not that important as the Word of God is not abundantly clear on that. The heart of the matter is that they are kept away.

The fundamental problem with the pre-trib resurrection is that it does not account for the saints beheaded for their faith during the great tribulation, as there are only two resurrections mentioned in scriptures. The first resurrection at the post-trib Rapture of all the saints to meet the

Lord in the air and the second resurrection after the millennium reign of Christ unto condemnation.

> 'And I saw thrones, and they sat on them, and judgment was committed to them. Then I saw the souls of those who had been beheaded for their witness to Jesus and for the word of God, who had not worshiped the beast or his image, and had not received his mark on their foreheads or on their hands. And they lived and reigned with Christ for a thousand years. But the rest of the dead did not live again until the thousand years were finished. This is the first resurrection. Blessed and holy is he who has part in the first resurrection. Over such the second death has no power, but they shall be priests of God and of Christ, and shall reign with Him a thousand years." [243]

The pre-trib school of thought creates a third resurrection of those beheaded for their faith during the great tribulation creating a third resurrection, one pre-trib, one post-trib and one post millennium. The word of God is clear that there are only two resurrections and the fact that his word is infallible we do well to take him at His word. Since the scriptures warn against adding to the word of God:

> "For I testify to everyone who hears the words of the prophecy of this book: If anyone adds to these things, God will add to him the plagues that are written in this book." [244]

All the saints agree on this, the blessed hope is that the overcomers will escape the great tribulation and that all the saints will be caught up to meet the Lord in the air at the pre-wrath rapture before the day of the Lord. They will be kept away from that hour of testing. God has everything under control.

The Apostle Paul says "behold I show you a mystery, a glorious secret," "we will not all sleep, we who are alive will be caught up to meet the Lord in the air." [245] The mystery is , "we will not all sleep", or be killed. The Antichrist will not be able to kill the overcomers. The saints will not be defeated. They will be victorious to the very end.

The Bible holds the key to the mystery of the last days. God designed everything in the universe to bless His children in time and throughout eternity. He predestined His elect for preservation in the last days. He will keep them away from the testing that is coming upon the whole world.

The Bible gives us the precedents of how He has taken care of His children in previous crises. He protected Israel in Goshen, Daniel in the lion's den, and Meshach, Shadrach and Abednego in the furnace.

Josephus, the historian, gives us an account of how the early church was kept away from the genocide and destruction of Jerusalem by Titus in 70 A.D. He said that not one of the followers of Jesus perished in Jerusalem. They moved to Petra and God protected them there. History provides us broad patterns of divine protection for His people in mortal danger.

God planned the fate of the earth. He has given us implicit rather than explicit details on this matter. God had His children in mind when he planned the endgame. He has told us enough so that we can know that there is a hiding place for His children, a place where no harm can come, in the midst of momentous terminal events under the shadow of the Almighty.

"He who dwells in the secret place of the Most High shall abide under the shadow of the Almighty. . . You shall not be afraid of the terror by night, nor of the arrow that flies by day, nor of the pestilence that walks in darkness, nor of the destruction that lays waste at noonday.

A thousand may fall at your side, and ten thousand at your right hand, but it shall not come near you. Only with your eyes shall you look, and see the reward of the wicked. Because you have made the LORD, who is my refuge, even the Most High, your dwelling place, no evil shall befall you, nor shall any plague come near your dwelling; for He shall give His angels charge over you, to keep you in all your ways." [246]

Biblical predictions of the end of days give hidden truth that will cause you to live victorious in the last days. We can face this period of climactic events of apocalyptic proportions with great confidence. We know the only hiding place is under the shadow of the Almighty.

The prophet Isaiah gives a clue, and not an answer, when he describes where the end time saints will be hidden during the climactic horrors "until the indignation is past."

> "Come, My people, enter your chambers, and shut your doors behind you; hide yourself, as it were for a little moment, until the indignation is past." [247]

The Lord will instruct the saints, "to enter into (their) chambers and close their doors behind (them) and hide for a little while (42 months of the great tribulation) until the indignation is past. "A thousand may fall at your side and ten thousand at your right hand, but it shall not approach you. You will only look and see the recompense of the wicked." Lot was hidden in his own chambers all night, as the Lord blinded the enemies who surrounded his house, trying to find the door.

In the predictions of the last days in the Daniel Messianic Clock catastrophic events are destined to happen, "such as never was since there was a nation, even to that same time." [248]

Contrary to what doomsayers teach concerning the great tribulation the prophet Daniel is also clear that during these ominous events and contemporaneous to the catastrophe, "the people that do know their God shall be strong and do exploits." [249] They will be immune from the attacks of the Antichrist. They will do great exploits.

The God in them is bigger than the Antichrist. They will walk in their sonship identity and destiny unhindered by the world. They will "do all things through Christ who strengthens them." [250]

The reason God tells us the end time events is not to scare us but to show us that He is in control. He will be with us. Jesus prayed for our protection till He comes to take us home.

> "I have given them your word; and the world hath hated them, because they are not of the world, even as I am not of the world. *I pray not that thou should take them out of the world, but that thou should keep them from the evil.* They are not of the world, even as I am not of the world. Sanctify them through thy truth: thy word is truth. As thou hast sent me into the world, even so have I also sent them into the world. And for their sakes I sanctify myself, that they also might be sanctified through the truth." [251]

He did not pray for us to be raptured away. He prayed "not that thou should take them out of the world, but that thou should keep them from the evil." He will keep the overcomers from evil during the great tribulation. He promised, "when the enemy comes like a flood he will raise up a standard." [252] The overcomers will be the standard God is going to raise up. They will be pillars in the storm for the people of God.

KEPT AWAY BEFORE BEING TAKEN AWAY

Immediately after the tribulation of those days the sun will be darkened, and the moon will not give its light; the stars will fall from heaven, and the powers of the heavens will be shaken. Then the sign of the Son of Man will appear in heaven, and then all the tribes of the earth will mourn, and they will see the Son of Man coming on the clouds of heaven with power and great glory.

> "He will send His angels with a great sound of a trumpet, and they will gather together His elect from the four winds, from one end of heaven to the other." [253] The world will be unprepared, the masses of lost humanity will not be looking for Christ, "For when they say, "Peace and

safety!" then sudden destruction comes upon them, as labor pains upon a pregnant woman. And they shall not escape." [254]

The Bible is clear the Church will be caught up to meet the Lord in the air and be gathered unto Him immediately after the tribulation of those days. The only question that the body of Christ debates is what happens to the saints without spot or wrinkle, the overcomers during the tribulation? He promised that they would be kept away from that hour of testing that will come upon the whole world. "Because you have kept My command to persevere, I also will keep you from the hour of trial which shall come upon the whole world, to test those who dwell on the earth."[255] This is the fundamental truth of the gospel, they are kept and hidden away, but not taken away until "immediately after the tribulation of those days".[256]

"You are of God, little children, and have overcome them, because He who is in you is greater than he who is in the world." [257]

The rapture is pre-wrath of God, which will be poured on the wicked immediately after the church is caught up to meet the Lord in the air. During the great tribulation the overcomers will be kept away from the wrath of the dragon and the Antichrist. He will shield the overcomers from the wrath of the dragon during the great tribulation. It should be noted that the wrath of the dragon after he is cast out of heaven is against Israel and the saints.

The wrath of God is against the dragon, the Antichrist and the wicked and it comes immediately after the saints have been removed from the earth. During the tribulation God has promised, "When you pass through the waters, I *will be* with you; And through the rivers, they shall not overflow you. When you walk through the fire, you shall not be burned, nor shall the flame scorch you." [258] God is a promise keeper.

He will keep them away from the evil one; the devil will not be able to touch the anointed of the Lord, the overcomers. They will be immune, safe and secure under the shadow of the Almighty. They will see the unprecedented natural disasters and witness the greatest carnage and nuclear holocaust, yet it will not affect them.

> "No weapon formed against you shall prosper, and every tongue *which* rises against you in judgment you shall condemn. This *is* the heritage of the servants of the LORD, and their righteousness *is* from Me," Says the LORD." [259]

There is no need to fear the great tribulation. It will not affect the overcomer. They will be kept away or taken away from the onslaught of the enemy. The compromised will go through the fire of the great tribulation to cleanse them and make them ready to meet the Lord in the air.

This gives a second chance to the compromised saints to be cleansed. It is a wonderful blessing because the "sufferings of this world cannot be compared with the glory that awaits the saints." [260]

> "Those who do wickedly against the covenant he shall corrupt with flattery; but the people who know their God shall be strong, and carry out *great exploits.* And those of the people who understand shall instruct many; yet *for many* days they shall fall by sword and flame, by captivity and plundering. Now when they fall, they shall be aided with a little help; but many shall join with them by intrigue. And *some* of those of understanding shall fall, to refine them, purify *them,* and make *them* white, *until* the time of the end; because *it is* still for the appointed time."
> [261]

What a day that will be! The pre-wrath rapture will take place before the end of the world and the Day of the Lord, when he pours His wrath on the wicked.

"For behold, the day is coming, burning like an oven, and all the proud, yes, all who do wickedly will be stubble. And the day which is coming shall burn them up," Says the LORD of hosts, "That will leave them neither root nor branch. But to you who fear My name the Sun of Righteousness shall arise with healing in His wings; And you shall go out and grow fat like stall-fed calves. You shall trample the wicked, for they shall be ashes under the soles of your feet on the day that I do *this,*" Says the LORD of hosts." [262]

After the battle of Armageddon, Israel will begin to cleanse the land from the wreckage of the battle. It will take them seven years. During that time the saints will be in heaven with Christ before his second coming with the saints to rule and reign for one thousand years from Jerusalem.

The battle of Armageddon and the war of Gog and Magog in Ezekiel 38 and 39 are one and the same. They both end up in what is known as the "supper of the Great God for the vultures. Ezekiel wrote:

"And as for you, son of man, thus says the Lord GOD, 'Speak to every sort of bird and to every beast of the field: Assemble yourselves and come; Gather together from all sides to My sacrificial meal which I am sacrificing for you, *a great sacrificial meal on the mountains of Israel,* that you may eat flesh and drink blood. You shall eat the flesh of the mighty, drink the blood of the princes of the earth, Of rams and lambs, Of goats and bulls, All of them fatlings of Bashan. You shall eat fat till you are full, And drink blood till you are drunk, At My sacrificial meal which I am sacrificing for you. You shall be filled at My table with horses and riders, with mighty men and with all the men of war," says the Lord GOD." [263]

John, in the book of Revelation, describes the same event "the supper of the Great God":

> "Then I saw an angel standing in the sun; and he cried with a loud voice, saying to all the birds that fly in the midst of heaven, "Come and gather together for the *supper of the great God that you may eat the flesh of kings*, the flesh of captains, the flesh of mighty men, the flesh of horses and of those who sit on them, and the flesh of all *people,* free and slave, both small and great." And I saw the beast, the kings of the earth, and their armies, gathered together to make war against Him who sat on the horse and against His army." [264]

It is important to note that Israel will take seven years after the Battle of Armageddon and the rapture preparing for the coming of the kingdom when Christ returns with his saints to rule.

> "Then those who dwell in the cities of Israel will go out and set on fire and burn the weapons, both the shields and bucklers, the bows and arrows, the javelins and spears; and they will make fires with them for seven years." [265]

The last seven years before the millennium rule of Christ is initiated by the rapture. Israel as the earthly seed of Abraham will begin to cleanse the land in anticipation of the Messianic Kingdom. The Church as the bride of Christ will be in heaven for the wedding feast before coming back with Christ to rule and reign with Him.

If you can grasp the full impact of the prophetic message contained in this book, you will realize you have nothing to be afraid of what is coming. Most Christians tune out end time prophecy out of fear; while others are hoodwinked into thinking it won't affect them.

coming. Most Christians tune out end time prophecy out of fear; while others are hoodwinked into thinking it won't affect them.

The basic point to be made is the foolish virgins did not make an extra preparation, "for the night comes when no man can work." [266] They missed their divine appointment with destiny while it was still day.

I believe this generation is standing at the precipice and the saints of God have a divine responsibility to prepare a generation of overcomers that will do exploits during the coming dark days. The pages of this book will help you to see current events in the light of Biblical prophecy.

The stage is being set up for the final drama. This is the stage that God has called you to do exploits according to Daniel's prediction, "they that know their God will do exploits." [267]

The best of your years is yet to come. Jesus said, "He that believeth on me, the works that I do shall he do also; and greater works than these shall he do; because I go unto my Father." [268] For a time such as this you came into the kingdom.

The future for this generation projected in Biblical prophecy is unparallel from the saints of all ages, they are destined to do greater exploits, multiplication of resources, going invisible in the presence of their enemies and being translated.

They will be kept away from the hour of testing, "which will come upon the entire world to try them that dwell on the earth." [269] God will open the fourth dimension for the overcomers. Jesus operated beyond the three-dimensional world during his earthly ministry. The endtime overcomers will step into that dimension and do many untold miracles, great exploits as predicted, "but the people that do know their God shall be strong, and do exploits." [270]

CHAPTER TWENTY-ONE

THE MANIFESTATION OF THE SONS OF GOD

God has prepared great and mighty things for his end time people. "things which eye has not seen nor ear heard and which have not entered into the heart of man." [271] This is a promise for these last days, yet most Christians believe that these unseen, unheard of and unthought of promises are revealed when we go to heaven.

The Apostle is clear as these things are revealed by the spirit and not by the way of the rapture or death. "But God hath revealed them unto us by his Spirit: for the Spirit searches all things, yea, the deep things of God." [272]

This is the generation the Prophet Daniel said, "those who know their God will do exploits." [273] The Apostle Paul speaks of a time when creation will be emancipated by the sons of God:

> "For the earnest expectation of the creation eagerly waits for the revealing of the sons of God. For the creation was subjected to futility, not willingly, but because of Him who subjected *it* in hope; because the creation itself also will be delivered from the bondage of corruption into the glorious liberty of the children of God." [274]

In these last days, the overcomers will enter the realm of unlimited anointing and glory. It is God's plan to pour out His spirit without measure upon all flesh in our day.

> "And it shall come to pass afterward, that I will pour out my spirit upon all flesh; and your sons and your daughters shall prophesy, your old men shall dream dreams, your young men shall see visions: And also upon the servants

and upon the handmaids in those days will I pour out my spirit." [275]

God is not going to close this Dispensation of Grace without the overcomers coming into the fullness of the spirit, which constitutes the real heritage of the saints. The heritage that has been preserved for us in these final days on earth is available for this generation. The promise remains for us to ask, believe and receive.

I feel in my heart that we must press forward with all diligence in the Spirit "counting not myself to have apprehended: but this one thing I do, forgetting those things which are behind, and reaching forth unto those things which are before." [276]

We have within us the potential inborn nature yet to be released "to the measure of the stature of the fullness of Christ." [277] It is not fully expressed because of the momentous spiritual battles we are yet to fight to emancipate the saints into their glorious liberty of the sons of God.

The sons of God are hindered from walking into the fullness of their sonship identity and heritage because of Satan's accusation before God night and day. When Satan is thrown out of heaven in these last days, the saints will rise and enter the realm of unlimited glory and the measure of the stature of the fullness of Christ.

"And war broke out in heaven: Michael and his angels fought with the dragon; and the dragon and his angels fought, but they did not prevail, nor was a place found for them in heaven any longer. So the great dragon was cast out, that serpent of old, called the Devil and Satan, who deceives the whole world; he was cast to the earth, and his angels were cast out with him.

Then I heard a loud voice saying in heaven, "Now salvation, and strength, and the kingdom of our God, and the power of His Christ have come, for the accuser of our brethren, who accused them before our God day and night, has been cast down. And they overcame him by the blood of the Lamb and by the word of their testimony, and they did not love their lives to the death. " [278]

The devil will soon be cast out of heaven and his accusation of the saints silenced forever. The overcomers will rise and cross over Jordan and possess the measure of the stature of the fullness of Christ and do great exploits.

The manifestation (apokalupsis) of the sons of God is the unveiling of Christ in us, who has made us more than conquerors. When the devil is thrown out of the exalted place in the heavenlies, the saints will ascend to the measure of the stature of the fullness of Christ.

When Michael the Archangel casts down Satan out of the heavenlies, "there will be no more condemnation to those that are in Christ Jesus who walk not after the flesh but after the spirit for the accuser of the brethren will be thrown out." [279] There will be a realization and full manifestation of our glorious liberty in Christ. "For the just shall walk by faith." [280]

Jesus entered the fourth dimension when the anointing came upon Him without measure upon all his flesh after John baptized him to fulfill the law. He was manifested (apokalupsis) to the world in his full sonship identity.

When God pours His spirit without measure on the overcomers in these last days they will be manifested in their full glory "for the earnest expectation of the creation" [281] is to be delivered from the corruption of this age. As the saints are the body of Christ who "fills all in all" [282] they will put the devil and his host under their feet as the body of Christ, his extension on earth.

The devil will be put under our feet before Jesus comes back as God promised: "The Lord said unto my Lord, sit then on my right hand, until I make thy foes they footstool" [283]

The overcomers will rise and apprehend the fullness of Him that fills all in all. They will possess the land of promise and restore all things that the devil had stolen from man in preparation of the return of Christ as King of Kings.

"And he shall send Jesus Christ, which before was preached unto you: *Whom heaven must receive until the times of restitution of all things*, which God hath spoken by the mouth of all his holy prophets since the world began." [284]

Jesus will not rapture a sick, naked, wretched, defeated church, but a church without spot or wrinkle, victorious and triumphant. He will remain in heaven until the times of restitution of all things, which God has spoken by the mouth of all his holy prophets since the world began: The rise of a mature sonship on earth to rule and reign over the kingdom of darkness. The place Satan is occupying in the heavenlies is a place prepared for the saints to reign. "For we are more than conquerors through Him who loved us." [285]

As Jesus received the fullness of his sonship authority at baptism the saints will enter that realm when Satan is cast out of heaven and cease his accusation of the saints before God night and day.

The picture of the victorious saints in the last days is wonderful beyond description. They will do great exploits and greater works than Jesus earthly ministry as He promised. The fourth dimension will be opened to them, the flood gates of the supernatural will be opened. "The gates of hell will not prevail over the church." [286]

Therefore as we contemplate the last days of earth time, we need to focus on the coming glory upon the overcomers and Angels on assignments. "Are they not all ministering spirits, sent forth to minister for them who shall be heirs of salvation." [287] God has provided a Heavenly bodyguard to watch over the overcomers.

We have the precedents of how an angel fed Elijah, an angel wiped out the Assyrian army by cutting off all the mighty men of valor, an Angel protected Elisha and blinded the eyes of his enemies, an angel protected Daniel in the lion's den, the angel delivered Peter from prison and the angel of the Lord was sent to John to give him the revelation of the end of days.

There will be more angelic visitation and ministration in these last days than any other time in history. All the past visitations were types and shadows of things to come in our days.

> "For He will command his angels concerning you to guard you in all your ways. They will lift you up in their hands to that you will not strike your foot against a stone." [288]

God sustained three million people, thousands of animals, for forty years in a great and terrible desert. He gave them meat to eat, manna from heaven and water from a rock. They lacked nothing, their shoes did not wear out. He shielded them from the desert heat with a cloud and warmed them in the cold nights of the desert by a pillar of fire over them.

Biblical eschatology is contrary to the concepts being taught the church. All they hear is the gloom and doom and not the glorious visitation from on high and vindication of the overcomers, without spot or wrinkle, undefiled by the world.

The glory of God and the divine potentiality that lies dormant within their DNA as sons of God will be released. As an egg contains the likeness inside of its kind, though one cannot see the similarity until the crusty covering is cracked open. So is the cocoon before the butterfly breaks out.

The saints have within them the incorruptible seed as partakers of the divine nature. "To an inheritance incorruptible, and undefiled, and that fades not away, reserved in heaven for you." [289] The hour has come in these final days on earth for the saints to break out and show forth the glories of Him that "called them out of the kingdom of darkness into the kingdom of his dear son." [290]

The Apostle Peter said Jesus will not come back until "the restitution of all things which God has spoken by the mouth of all his holy prophets since the world began." [291]

The earthly minded Christians, who sit back in ease and self-complacency awaiting an easy way out, will not rapture but capture. They don't realize that God brought them out to bring them into the heritage of the saints in Christ, the kingdom of God within them and to be conformed to His image. They are world conformers and not transformers. They are ignorant of the season of their visitation.

We who have come to the end of the ages have been promised the restoration of the glory of the past ages. They cannot comprehend these things therefore they cannot appropriate them.

The remnant will enter boldly into the throne of grace and posses their glorious heritage in the spirit, the full attributes of their sonship. They will comprehend and appropriate all the riches of their calling as promised. "May be able to comprehend with all saints what is the breadth, and length, and depth, and height; And to know the love of Christ, which passes knowledge, that ye might be filled with all the fullness of God." [292] When the devil is cast out of heaven God has a surprise waiting for him down here on earth: A transcended Church.

The saints will enter into the realm of glory unparallel in history. The glory shield will cover them they will appropriate the fullness of their sonship nature as sons of God. They will go and preach everywhere, "the Lord working with them confirming the word with signs following." [293]

They will confront the forces of evil, they will fight the fire of hell, with the fire from above. They will overcome the devil "by the blood of the lamb and by the word of their testimony and they love not their lives unto death" [294]

Contrary to the widespread teaching that the saints will flee away into safety when the cosmic conflict begins, they will fight and overcome the forces of evil. The truth is that the Lord will remain seated at the right hand of God until the manifested sons of God defeat the devil and they put their feet on the neck of the devil.

> "For David is not ascended into the heavens: but he says himself, The Lord said unto my Lord, Sit thou on my right hand, until I make thy foes thy footstool." [295]

Jesus will stay in heaven at the right hand of God until God working through the saints undefiled, holy and happy, demonstrate to the world the power of the risen Christ. The devil is defeated. Jesus said, "It is finished." [296] There is nothing to worry about.

> "We are more than conquerors through Christ who strengthens us." [297]

The restoration of all things will bring the saints into full identification with Christ. He is the vine and we are the branches. The vine shares its life with the branches.

> "I am the true vine, and My Father is the vinedresser. Every branch in Me that does not bear fruit He takes away; and every *branch* that bears fruit He prunes, that it may bear more fruit. You are already clean because of the word which I have spoken to you. Abide in Me, and I in you. As the branch cannot bear fruit of itself, unless it abides in the vine, neither can you, unless you abide in Me.
> I am the vine, you *are* the branches. He who abides in Me, and I in him, bears much fruit; for without Me you can do nothing." [298]

Jesus is the whole vine, root, stack, branches, leaves and fruit. Jesus is clearly saying he is one with his body. We are the expression of the "fullness of him that fills all in all." [299]

The overcomers in these final days of the Dispensation of Grace are striving to grow into the fullness of Christ and perfection as exhorted by the Apostle Paul;

> "Till we all come in the unity of the faith, and of the knowledge of the Son of God, unto a perfect man, unto the measure of the stature of the fullness of Christ." [300]

It is attaining the fullness of Christ that will usher in the demonstration of what the "eye has not seen, the ear has not heard and what has not entered into the heart of man." [301] Oh, what a grand and glorious day that awaits the overcomers in our terminal generation.

The manifestation of the mature sons of God will be far beyond man's highest imagination, infinitely far above all that we would ask or think. They will be able to explore the eternal recesses of the deep things of the Spirit and rise to unfathomable heights of His glory far above Satan's domain. They will be empowered to do greater miracles than Jesus did when He was on earth. Jesus said, "Greater miracles than these shall you do." [302] Daniel says concerning this generation, "They that know their God shall do exploits." [303]

The manifested sons of God share the same nature as Christ. The Adamic nature is crucified with Christ. The cross of Jesus terminates the old nature. They are born again from above. They now have the nature of the second Adam.

> "And so it is written, the first man Adam was made a living soul; the last Adam was made a quickening spirit. Howbeit that was not first which is spiritual, but that which is natural; and afterward that which is spiritual.
> The first man is of the earth, earthy; the second man is the Lord from heaven. As is the earthy, such are they also that are earthy: and as is the heavenly, such are they also that are heavenly. And as we have borne the image of the earthy, we shall also bear the image of the heavenly." [304]

Our Adamic image has been replaced by our new Christ like image, "And as we have borne the image of the earthy, we shall also bear the image of the heavenly." [305] The manifest sons of God will come into the fullness of Christ and reflect His transcended image and glory.

The second Adam is a life giving spirit, creative, victorious and triumphant, such is the heritage of those in Christ. They bear the image of the heavenly. The devil cannot defeat those who bear the full image of the heavenly. They resist the devil and he flees from them. The fiery darts of the enemy cannot penetrate the glory of God upon the overcomers because they will know His love that surpasses knowledge and be filled to the measure of the fullness of God." [306]

This is a conquering generation that will restore all things before Christ comes back as heaven must receive him "until the time of restitution of all things which God has spoken by the mouth of all his holy prophets since the world began." [307]

There is no limit to the measure of the power, which the saints in these last days may appropriate. The limitations are that they themselves choose in unbelief, "as all things are possible to them that believe." [308]

In this we are confident that before the end of the church age a company of overcomers will rise and appropriate, even here and now their glorious heritage as manifest sons of God bearing the full image of Christ. It is only then "that which the palmerworm hath left hath the locust eaten; and that which the locust hath left hath the cankerworm eaten; and that which the cankerworm hath left hath the caterpillar eaten, shall be restored." [309]

All the prayers of the saints of the bygone ages, are to find their fulfillment in this great hour. The overcomers in our day will receive the glory as Jesus prayed, "the glory which you gave me I have given them, that they may be one, even as we are one." [310]

We should expect that in these last shabuwas or sabbatical cycles before the end of days, the great exploits foretold in Daniel would happen. In ages past they happened in a small scale in types and shadow, now in fullness. The immensities of these exploits will make this the most glorious days to be alive. There must arise a group of overcomers who shall defeat the kingdom of darkness completely, before this dispensation draws to a close.

The glorious manifestation of the sons of God in these last days has been completely lost and obscured amidst the gloom and doom of the great tribulation teachings. What does this mean? The Christians are scared, they want out, rather than being excited of the coming glory and vindication of the sons of God. The sons of wickedness will no longer have dominion over the saints.

The manifest sons of God will take the whole gospel of the kingdom to the whole world before the end in fulfillment of the great commission. "And this gospel of the kingdom shall be preached in all the world for a witness unto all nations; and then shall the end come." [311] This is an unfinished task of the kingdom. The manifest sons of God will accomplish this urgent mission impossible in our day.

The mystery of the coming glory of the manifested sons of God in these last days is too much for us to comprehend. God promises to do the unthinkable, the unimaginable, the unattainable, "what the eye has not seen, the ear has not heard nor has it entered into the heart of man in these last days." [312] God is going to speak to this generation as He did in ages past.

> "Whose voice then shook the earth: but now he hath promised, saying, Yet once more I shake not the earth only, but also heaven." [313]

This coming shaking will displace Satan and his hosts from the heavenly places where the devil accuses the saints night and day. The devil will be thrown out, he will cease his accusation of the saints, and it is in these days that those that know their God will shake the world with extraordinary miracles, signs and wonders. The world has not seen anything yet, the best of the kingdom of God is yet to come before the rapture.

The doors to countries, which have been closed to missionary enterprise, will be burst open by the coming "perfect man, unto the stature of the fullness of Christ." [314] The manifest Sons of God. The overcomers! Though they will not be able to take every person to Christ, they will be able to take Christ to every person to make a choice. They are heralds of His coming, messengers of the coming King of Kings. They are unstoppable. "The gates of hell will not prevail." [315] Jesus the King of Kings has given the saints a royal mandate:

"Behold, I give unto you power to tread on serpents and scorpions, and over all the power of the enemy: and nothing shall by any means hurt you." [316]

The Lord will shorten the days for the sake of the elect, not because they will be in danger of being killed by the Antichrist. He will shorten the days to save mankind from being wiped out. The elect are appointed to rule the nations with a rod of iron. God does not want the nations to be wiped out for the sake of the elect to take over. He will suddenly come for His saints.

THE GREATEST HARVEST OF ALL TIME

The period of the greatest persecution of the saints will be the time of the greatest harvest in the history of the church. The church will experience abundant joy in tribulation as they triumph over opposition. History has shown us that the church is at its best under attack. The overcomers need to look up with joyful anticipation for the most spectacular endtime harvest, "multitudes, multitudes in the valley of decision." [317]

The church needs to cast aside the gloom and doom eschatology of defeat. God is in control of the endgame. It is time to ascertain the truth that the church is destined to rise above the onslaught of the enemy. "When the enemy comes in like a flood, the Spirit of the LORD will lift up a standard against him." [318] The endtime constitutes a period of unprecedented outpouring of the Holy Spirit. It is a time of double blessings, double anointing, double revelation and supreme glory of God upon the saints.

"Be glad then, you children of Zion, And rejoice in the LORD your God; For He has given you the former rain faithfully, and He will cause the rain to come down for you. The former rain, and the latter rain in the first month." [319]

We have arrived at the appointed time for the greatest ingathering of lost souls:

"Behold, the days are coming, says the LORD, When the plowman shall overtake the reaper, And the treader of grapes him who sows seed; The mountains shall drip with sweet wine, And all the hills shall flow with it." [320]

Destiny is not a matter of chance it is a matter of choice. The saints need to make earnest commitment to renew their vision for soul winning and visualize the great harvest in these last days, to bring in the fullness of the Gentiles. The church must stop conditioning the saints for defeat with the gloom and doom teaching regarding the great tribulation. The Bible teaches the eschatology of victory and triumph over the forces of darkness. "Greater is He that is in us than He that is in the world." [321]

The pessimist and defeatist teaching about the end of day's destruction of the Church is Satan's tactic to scare the saints. He is a liar and He is defeated. "We are more than conquerors through Him who loved us." [322] The eschatology of defeat ignores God's promises, His amazing grace, boundless love and sustaining grace. "He that called you is faithful, He will keep you." [323]

Before us is an open door that no man can shut, the outpouring of the former and latter rain all at once; Unprecedented anointing! It is time for that greatest harvest, "the plowman shall overtake the reaper and the treader of the grapes him that sows seed." [324] This generation will break the time barrier and fulfill the words of Jesus "that this gospel of the kingdom shall be preached in all the world for a witness unto all nations, and then shall the end come." [325]

CHAPTER TWENTY- TWO

THE MESSIANIC CLOCK: THE RAPTURE

The saints will be caught up to meet the Lord in the air. This is the blessed hope of every child of God. Jesus will come back to take his saints in the same manner He ascended to heaven, bodily and visibly as described in the book of Acts:

> "And when he had spoken these things, while they beheld, he was taken up; and a cloud received him out of their sight. And while they looked steadfastly toward heaven as he went up, behold, two men stood by them in white apparel; Which also said, you men of Galilee, why stand gazing up into heaven? This same Jesus, which is taken up from you into heaven, shall so come in like manner as ye have seen him go into heaven." [326]

The pre-wrath rapture of the saints lies at the core of the gospel. Jesus died to redeem a people from the earth to share with Him His glory and kingdom for eternity. The invitation is to whosoever, whenever and wherever that accepts Jesus Christ as personal Savior. He will be caught away when the trumpet sounds and the saints are called to meet him in the air. This is how the Apostle Paul describes this glorious event:

> "For the Lord Himself will descend from heaven with a shout, with the voice of an archangel, and with the trumpet of God. And the dead in Christ will rise first. Then we who are alive *and* remain shall be caught up together with them in the clouds to meet the Lord in the air. And thus we shall always be with the Lord." [327]

This blessed event is closer than it has ever been. I believe in the rapture, the dead in Christ shall be raised and we who are alive will be caught up to meet the Lord in the air. We are living in the days when this passage of scripture could be fulfilled any day in our time.

> "Assuredly, I say to you, there are some standing here who shall not taste death till they see the Son of Man coming in His kingdom." [328]

We are living in a time when all the signs of the times are being fulfilled. One of these days suddenly our work on earth will be over, the King of Kings will appear in the eastern sky and the saints will be caught up to meet Him in the air for the wedding feast of the Lamb. The Church is the bride of Christ and He is the bridegroom.

The Wedding Feast will last seven years, the saints will receive the rewards and every man's work will be tried by fire. The Apostle Paul exhorts the believers to fight the good fight of faith to run the race and to finish the course. There is no dispute the hour is late; it is time to actualize the will of God in our lives and not to be complacent. Like the Apostle Paul every believer must have the same passion and heart:

> "Not that I have already attained, or am already perfected; but I press on, that I may lay hold of that for which Christ Jesus has also laid hold of me. Brethren, I do not count myself to have apprehended; but one thing I do, forgetting those things which are behind and reaching forward to those things which are ahead, I press toward the goal for the prize of the upward call of God in Christ Jesus." [329]

The mark of our high calling is to be conformed to His image and be ready for the rapture to meet the Lord in the air. Jesus Christ is coming back to take the saints without spot or wrinkle away in a twinkling of an eye, before He pours his wrath on earth. The saints have been forgiven and are free from the wrath of God. We are not appointed unto wrath.

"For God did not appoint us to wrath, but to obtain salvation through our Lord Jesus Christ." [330]

IMMINENT RETURN OF CHRIST

The rapture of the saints to meet the Lord in the air is a distinct event from the Second Coming of Christ. The first coming (rapture) is for the saints, and the second coming is with the saints to set up the millennium kingdom. There is a seven-year period during which the Wedding Feast of the Lamb, and the judgment seat of Christ occur, before He returns to set up His Kingdom for a thousand years on earth.

For the first time in history all the signs of the time are aligned for any moment return of Jesus. The scriptures give us very specific signs to look for before the rapture. They are all fulfilled or are being fulfilled in our very eyes.

> "Now learn this parable from the fig tree: When its branch has already become tender and puts forth leaves, you know that summer is near. So you also, when you see all these things, know that it is near—at the doors! Assuredly, I say to you, this generation will by no means pass away till all these things take place. Heaven and earth will pass away, but My words will by no means pass away. " [331]

Jesus said, "when you shall see all these things know that it is near, even at the door." [332] This is the first generation to see all things prophesied to take place before Jesus comes back for his saints any moment. He is near even at the door. The timeline has been shortened. We are living in a prophetic spectrum of any moment return of Christ. Eternity has already broken into this age.

All too often there is confusion among the saints regarding the Rapture and the Second Coming of Christ. In the preceding pages we will discuss the two events in detail. It must be noticed that the grand finale is when Jesus comes back with the saints to rule the earth, for a thousand years.

There are no signs preceding that event. The devil is already defeated. The Antichrist and the false prophet are already thrown into the lake of fire during the time of the battle of Armageddon and the Day of the Lord.

Every generation is taught watch (paratereo) and be ready (paralambano) to be received unto Him. Since heaven's doors are continually opened to the saints who are called to depart to be with the Lord. At any moment. To be absent from this body is to be present with the Lord.

> "For we know that if our earthly house of this tabernacle were dissolved, we have a building of God, a house not made with hands, eternal in the heavens. Therefore we are always confident, knowing that, whilst we are at home in the body, we are absent from the Lord: For we walk by faith, not by sight:) We are confident, I say, and willing rather to be absent from the body, and to be present with the Lord." [333]

Although death is certain its timing is uncertain, it behooves every believer to be ready any moment to meet the Lord; "for to be absent from this body is to be present with the Lord." [334]

> "Then I heard a voice from heaven saying to me, Write: Blessed are the dead who die in the Lord from now on. Yes, says the Spirit, that they may rest from their labors, and their works follow them." [335]

We live in the imminent, any moment a sudden call to be with the Lord can come and we enter the rest from our labors. We cannot postpone our preparedness to meet the Lord. Any moment, in the twinkling of an eye, whether He calls us in death or He comes for us in the rapture we must be ready. We must live each day as if it were our last day.

WRATH OF GOD

It should be observed that after the saints are caught away to meet the Lord in the air that the wrath of God would be poured on the Antichrist and the wicked. The great whore is judged, mystery Babylon is fallen. The bowls of God's wrath are poured out:

First bowl, loathsome sores
Second and Third bowls, water is turned into blood
Fourth bowl, intense heat
Fifth bowl, blackness and darkness over the beast kingdom
Sixth bowl, Euphrates River is dried up for the Kings of the
    East to gather together for the Battle of Armageddon.

Now comes the grand finale, Christ comes with the host of heaven to fight against the Antichrist armies.

"Now I saw heaven opened, and behold, a white horse. And He who sat on him was called Faithful and True, and in righteousness He judges and makes war. His eyes were like a flame of fire, and on His head were many crowns. He had a name written that no one knew except Himself. He was clothed with a robe dipped in blood, and His name is called The Word of God.

And the armies in heaven, clothed in fine linen, white and clean followed Him on white horses. Now out of His mouth goes a sharp sword, that with it He should strike the nations. And He Himself will rule them with a rod of iron. He Himself treads the winepress of the fierceness and wrath of Almighty God.

And He has on His robe and on His thigh a name written: Then I saw an angel standing in the sun; and he cried with a loud voice, saying to all the birds that fly in the midst of heaven,

Come and gather together for the supper of the great God that you may eat the flesh of kings, the flesh of captains, the flesh of mighty men, the flesh of horses and of those who sit on them, and the flesh of all people, free and slave, both small and great. And I saw the beast, the kings of the earth, and their armies, gathered together to make war against Him who sat on the horse and against His army.

Then the beast was captured, and with him the false prophet who worked signs in his presence, by which he deceived those who received the mark of the beast and those who worshiped his image. These two were cast alive into the lake of fire burning with brimstone. And the rest were killed with the sword, which proceeded from the mouth of Him who sat on the horse. And all the birds were filled with their flesh." [336]

SECOND COMING OF CHRIST

The Second Coming of Christ is a distinct event separate from the Rapture. The Rapture is when Christ comes for the saints and the second coming is when He comes with the saints, seven years after the Rapture to set up the millennium kingdom on earth.

He will come the second time, in like manner that the Apostles saw him go into heaven. He was taken up, in a cloud of witness, the first fruit of the resurrected saints who were raised after his crucifixion. He took them to paradise in the third heaven. He went up from the Mount of Olives. He will return in like manner to the Mount of Olives with all the saints that were caught up to meet the Lord in the air. His feet will touch down again on the Mount of Olives.

"And his feet shall stand in that day upon the mount of Olives, which is before Jerusalem on the east, and the mount of Olives shall cleave in the midst thereof toward the east and toward the west, and there shall be a very great valley; and half of the mountain shall remove toward the north, and half of it toward the south." [337]

Isaiah's prophecy harmonizes with Zechariah regarding the second coming of Christ to Mount Zion as the long waited for redeemer of Israel.

"And the Redeemer shall come to Zion, and unto them that turn from transgression in Jacob, says the LORD." [338]

The prophet Zechariah identifies the Messiah of Israel as Jesus Christ, whom they crucified.

"And I will pour upon the house of David, and upon the inhabitants of Jerusalem, the spirit of grace and of supplications: and they shall look upon me whom they have pierced, and they shall mourn for him, as one mourns for his only son, and shall be in bitterness for him, as one that is in bitterness for his firstborn." [339]

The horrendous plagues, persecutions and demonic assaults, political upheaval and social confusion will consummate into a glorious coming "parousia" of Christ as King of Kings and Lord of Lords to set up His millennium reign

MESSIANIC PREDICTIONS

Two Comings of the Messiah
PROPHECIES CONCERNING CHRIST'S COMING

FULFILLED PROPHECIES	FUTURE PROPHECIES
First Coming	Second Coming
Isaiah 9:1-2 Isaiah 9:6 Isaiah 52:13 Isaiah 53-55:13 Isaiah 59:16-176 Isaiah 61:1-2a Zechariah 9:9 Isaiah 11:1-3 Jeremiah 23:5 Psalms 22:1-21 Psalms 3:1 Psalms 4:2 Genesis 49:10a Deuteronomy 18:15a-18 Zechariah 3:8 Psalms 2:7 Hebrews 1:5 Hebrews 5:5	Isaiah 9:3-5 Isaiah 9:7 Isaiah 56:1-8 Isaiah 59:17c-21 Isaiah 61:2b-11 Zechariah 9:10 Isaiah 11:4-9 Jeremiah 23:6-8 Psalms 22:22-31 Psalms 3:2-3 Psalms 4:1-3 Psalms 4:5-6 Genesis 49:106 Deuteronomy 4:18, 15b, 19 Zechariah 3:9-10 Psalms 2:8 I Thessalonians 2 Revelations 2:26-27 Revelations 21:2

CHAPTER TWENTY-THREE

THE MILLENNIUM KINGDOM

When Christ comes back with the saints He will establish the millennium reign on earth at the consummation of history of the fall of man. Satan will be bound and cast into the bottomless pit.

> "And I saw an angel come down from heaven, having the key of the bottomless pit and a great chain in his hand. And he laid hold on the dragon, that old serpent, which is the Devil, and Satan, and bound him a thousand years, And cast him into the bottomless pit, and shut him up, and set a seal upon him, that he should deceive the nations no more, till the thousand years should be fulfilled: and after that he must be loosed a little season." [340]

How thrilling it is to know that at the wrap up (sunteleia) of this present history of suffering the saints will reign on earth with Christ for a thousand years and there will be no more sorrow or pain.

> "Blessed and holy is he that hath part in the first resurrection: on such the second death hath no power, but they shall be priests of God and of Christ, and shall reign with him a thousand years." [341]

The earth will be restored to its original beauty and glory. There will be no more seas.

> "And he that sat upon the throne said, Behold, I make all things new. And he said unto me, write: for these words are true and faithful." [342]

The drama that started at the dawn of time in the garden of Eden, the drama of the ages, that defined all of history; the fall of man, the pain, the suffering and death will culminate in a cataclysmic grand finale battle of Armageddon. The Antichrist and the False Prophet will be cast into the lake of fire; the Devil bound and cast out into the bottomless pit. The Wedding Feast of the Lamb and the One Thousand Year Reign of Christ and the Saints will begin.

THE NEW HEAVEN AND NEW EARTH

In accordance with the Genesis Time template, the seventh day was set apart as a Sabbath rest. The seventh millennium is the Sabbath rest, and at the end of the One Thousand Year Reign of Christ, Satan will be loosed.

> "And when the thousand years are expired, Satan shall be loosed out of his prison, And shall go out to deceive the nations which are in the four quarters of the earth, Gog, and Magog, to gather them together to battle: the number of whom is as the sand of the sea. And they went up on the breadth of the earth, and compassed the camp of the saints about, and the beloved city: and fire came down from God out of heaven, and devoured them.
>
> And the devil that deceived them was cast into the lake of fire and brimstone, where the beast and the false prophet are, and shall be tormented day and night forever and ever." [343]

The devil will try again to fight God for the last time. This event will take place at the termination of one thousand year reign of Christ, seven thousand years cumulative from creation. This present heaven and earth will go into super nova. The Apostle Peter says this concerning our present planetary system.

"But the heavens and the earth, which are now, by the same word are kept in store, reserved unto fire against the Day of Judgment and perdition of ungodly men." [344]

But the day of the Lord will come as a thief in the night; in which the heavens shall pass away with a great noise, and the elements shall melt with fervent heat, the earth also and the works that are therein shall be burned up.
Seeing then that all these things shall be dissolved, what manner of persons ought ye to be in all holy conversation and godliness, Looking for and hasting unto the coming of the day of God, wherein the heavens being on fire shall be dissolved, and the elements shall melt with fervent heat."
[345]

As a fellow time traveler, we have come to the final judgment, the great White throne judgment of God. This is how John describes the proceedings of the final judgment of the wicked at the end of time in the book of Revelation;

"And I saw a great white throne, and him that sat on it, from whose face the earth and the heaven fled away; and there was found no place for them. And I saw the dead, small and great, stand before God; and the books were opened: and another book was opened, which is the book of life: and the dead were judged out of those things which were written in the books, according to their works. And the sea gave up the dead which were in it; and death and hell delivered up the dead which were in them: and they were judged every man according to their works. And death and hell were cast into the lake of fire.
This is the second death. And whosoever was not found written in the book of life was cast into the lake of fire." [346]

This marks the consummation of the ages, the end of this present creation. The ultimate future has arrived, eternity! God will create the New Heaven and the New Earth.

> "And I saw a new heaven and a new earth: for the first heaven and the first earth were passed away; and there was no more sea. And I John saw the holy city, New Jerusalem, coming down from God out of heaven, prepared as a bride adorned for her husband.
> And I heard a great voice out of heaven saying, Behold, the tabernacle of God is with men, and he will dwell with them, and they shall be his people, and God himself shall be with them, and be their God. And God shall wipe away all tears from their eyes; and there shall be no more death, neither sorrow, nor crying, neither shall there be any more pain: for the former things are passed away. And he that sat upon the throne said,
> Behold, I make all things new. And he said unto me, write for these words are true and faithful. And he said unto me, It is done. I am Alpha and Omega, the beginning and the end. I will give unto him that is athirst of the fountain of the water of life freely." [347]

THE NEW JERUSALEM

It is impossible to exaggerate the unspeakable glory that awaits the saints in the New Heaven and New Earth. The prophets saw down the passage of time and could not adequately describe what they saw.

> "And I saw a new heaven and a new earth: for the first heaven and the first earth were passed away; and there was no more sea. And I John saw the holy city, New Jerusalem, coming down from God out of heaven, prepared as a bride adorned for her husband." [348]

"And he carried me away in the spirit to a great and high mountain, and showed me that great city, the holy Jerusalem, descending out of heaven from God, Having the glory of God: and her light was like unto a stone most precious, even like a jasper stone, clear as crystal;

And had a wall great and high, and had twelve gates, and at the gates twelve angels, and names written thereon, which are the names of the twelve tribes of the children of Israel: On the east three gates; on the north three gates; on the south three gates; and on the west three gates. And the wall of the city had twelve foundations, and in them the names of the twelve apostles of the Lamb." [349]

"But I saw no temple in it, for the Lord God Almighty and the Lamb are its temple. The city had no need of the sun or of the moon to shine in it, for the glory of God illuminated it. The Lamb *is* its light. And the nations of those who are saved shall walk in its light, and the kings of the earth bring their glory and honor into it. Its gates shall not be shut at all by day there shall be no night there. And they shall bring the glory and the honor of the nations into it. But there shall by no means enter it anything that defiles, or causes an abomination or a lie, but only those who are written in the Lamb's Book of Life." [350]

It is important to observe that the Glory of God illuminates the city. The Lamb is the Light. There shall by no means enter it anything that defiles or causes an abomination. Words are inadequate to describe the magnificence of the Holy City paved with pure gold where the saints of Jesus Christ will spend eternity. The sufferings of this world cannot be compared to the Glory that awaits us.

This is the city Abraham looked for whose Maker and Builder is God. The streets will be paved of pure gold as pure as glass, transparent but opaque, one can see through its clear depth as you walk on it. It will be decorated with every kind of precious stone.

"Then He who sat on the throne said, "Behold, I make all things new." And He said to me, "Write, for these words are true and faithful." And He said to me, "It is done! I am the Alpha and the Omega, the Beginning and the End. I will give of the fountain of the water of life freely to him who thirsts. He who overcomes shall inherit all things, and I will be his God and he shall be My son." [351]

WHEN SHALL THE END OF THESE WONDERS BE?

O my Lord, what shall be the end of these things? (Daniel 12:8)

Commencement	Biblical Event	The End
4026 B.C.	Genesis Time Template: 6 days, 6,000 years from Creation. *Tells the end from the beginning.* (Isaiah 46:10) 1000 x 6 = 6,000 years	2026 A.D.
4026 B.C.	The Noahian time template: 120 Jubilee Years from Creation. *As it was in the Days of Noah.* (Matthew 24:37) 50 x 120 = 6,000 years	2026 A.D.
2026 B.C.	The Sodom and Gomorrah Template *As it was in the days of Lot.* (Luke 17:28)	2026 A.D.
600 B.C.	1,290 years from Destruction of the First Temple to the Erection of the *Abomination of Desolation.* (Daniel 12:11) (600 + 1,290) plus year zero	691 A.D.
691 A.D.	1,335 Years from the Abomination of Desolation, Dome of the Rock, to the Messianic Kingdom. (Daniel 12:12) (691 + 1335)	2026 A.D.
1536 A.D.	490 years from the Second Decree by Suleiman the Magnificent to Restore Jerusalem to the Messianic Kingdom. (Daniel 9:24) (1536 + 490)	2026 A.D.
2012	69th week of Daniel from the Issuing of the Second Decree by Suleiman the Magnificent to Restore Jerusalem. (Daniel 9:25)	2012-2019 A.D.
2019 Last seven years	70th week of Daniel from the issuing of the Second Decree by Suleiman the Magnificent to Restore Jerusalem. (Daniel 9:24) God will Finish the Transgression, make an end of sin. Make Reconciliation for Iniquity to Bring in Everlasting Righteousness. Seal the Vision and Prophecy and Anoint the Most Holy. Daniel 9:24 Messianic Advent	2019-2026 A.D.
2026	The Millennium Reign of Christ, (Revelation 20:6)	3026 A.D.
3026 A.D.	New Heaven and New Earth Revelation 21 Eternity Begins	

CONCLUSION

Seeing we are living in the terminal generation what can we do? Jesus gives us the answer. We must not retire like what happened in the past but refire. He said: "Occupy till I come." [352] We must continue to do business as usual but in an unusual spirit of excellence, with a heightened commitment to holy living.

This is the time to broaden your vision, to save the lost and to have a keen focus on the Kingdom of God by prioritizing spending time with Him: Accentuating your vision, optimizing your giving, maximizing your kingdom agenda and celebrating your family and friends. Simplifying your lifestyle, widening your circle of kingdom influence by expanding your fellowship with the saints. Enlarging your knowledge of the Word of God to impact your world by your words and deeds. Focusing on your God-given mission in life by using the talents God gave you for His Glory. Making God the only purpose for your life not making Him just number one, but making Him the only one. Becoming mission driven. This is how you prepare to prosper in this age of chaos and consummation.

I feel constrained by the Lord as one of the least of the brethren to be faithful to share these mysteries that have been hidden through the ages, as He has opened my spiritual eyes to decipher the revelation cryptogram. He has given me the grace to decode the enigma, crack the Daniel code, break the seal and uncover the mysteries and unravel the paradigm of the ages. God has promised He would reveal this sealed enigma in the last days.

God wants his children to anticipate the end time events and to take extra oil like the five wise virgins and build their houses on the rock before the perfect storm of the age's hits. The implications are ominous. This is a defining moment in history. As it was in the days of Noah so shall it be, he prepared by divine revelation.

God has a personalized and individualized destiny for each one of us in these last days. Stay in the mainstream red-hot for Jesus as a witness, finish college, and make wise investments by divine guidance. Go into business, get married and enjoy abundant life in Christ. Your future is in God's hand. Seek God's will for your life's end time assignment. Your protection is staying at the center of God's will. His will, his bill, his vision, his provision. God is fixing to do exploits through you in these last days. The game is not over yet! The super bowl has just begun. Do not be a spectator but prepare to be a player in the endgame.

It is not time to panic but to press forward to serve God more than ever before. I believe in the eschatology of victory for the people of God. I believe the best is yet to come. Jesus said, "not a hair of your head will perish." [353]

As God prospered the children of Israel in Egypt while the rest of the inhabitants were being judged. He has a Goshen provision for His saints who put their trust in Him in these perilous days. He is preparing to prosper and protect his children in these last days when they abide in Him as He Promised in His word for those who love him. This is the future number to call Psalms ninety-one. (91-1-11)

> "He who dwells in the secret place of the Most High Shall abide under the shadow of the Almighty. I will say of the LORD, *He is* my refuge and my fortress; My God, in Him I will trust. Surely He shall deliver you from the snare of the fowler *and* from the perilous pestilence.
> He shall cover you with His feathers, and under His wings you shall take refuge; His truth *shall be your* shield and buckler. You shall not be afraid of the terror by night, *Nor* of the arrow *that* flies by day, *Nor* of the pestilence *that* walks in darkness, *Nor* of the destruction *that* lays waste at noonday.
> A thousand may fall at your side, and ten thousand at your right hand; *But* it shall not come near you. Only with your eyes shall you look, and see the reward of the wicked. Because you have made the LORD, *who is* my refuge, *Even*

the Most High, your dwelling place, No evil shall befall you, Nor shall any plague come near your dwelling; For He shall give His angels charge over you, to keep you in all your ways." [354]

THE WAY OF SALVATION

Because of sin, you are separated from God.

> "For all have sinned and fall short of the glory of God." [355]

The penalty for your sin is death.

> "For the wages of sin *is* death, but the gift of God *is* eternal life in Christ Jesus our Lord." [356]

Jesus paid for the penalty for your sin.

> "But God demonstrates His own love toward us, in that while we were still sinners, Christ died for us." [357]

If you repent of your sin right now and then confess and trust Jesus Christ as your Lord and Savior, you will be saved from sin.

> For *"whoever calls on the name of the LORD shall be saved."* [358]
>
> "If you confess with your mouth the Lord Jesus and believe in your heart that God has raised Him from the dead, you will be saved." [359]

The assurance of your salvation:

> "Whoever believes that Jesus is the Christ is born of God." [360]
>
> "These things I have written to you who believe in the name of the Son of God, that you may know that you have eternal life, and that you may *continue to* believe in the name of the Son of God." [361]

Here is the Prayer of Salvation for you to pray to receive Jesus Christ as your Savior:

"O God my Father, I repent of all my sins. I acknowledge that I have sinned against you, I accept your son, Jesus Christ, as my personal Savior. I ask you to forgive my sins and to wash me clean by your precious blood. Come into my heart and be my Lord and Savior. Write my name in the book of life. Put your spirit within me to lead and guide me from this day forth. I confess you as my Lord and Savior. Please help me to understand your Word in the Bible, in Jesus name I pray Amen.

SCRIPTURE INDEX

Introduction

[1] Luke 8:17
[2] Daniel 12:9
[3] Daniel 12:10
[4] Amos 3:7
[5] 1 Thessalonians 5:4
[6] Genesis 6:3
[7] Matthew 24:22
[8] Deuteronomy 30:3
[9] Mark 13:23
[10] Acts 8:9-10
[11] Matthew 24:4-5
[12] 2 Chronicles 20:15b
[13] Daniel 12:9-10
[14] 1 Thessalonians 5:4-5
[15] 1 Thessalonians 5:4
[16] Revelation 1:1-3
[17] 1 Thessalonians 5:21
[18] Revelation 1:3
[19] 2 Chronicles 7:14
[20] Genesis 18:31,28
[21] 2 Chronicles 34: 24-28
[22] 2 Chronicles 36: 12, 14-17, 21
[23] Revelation 3: 15-22
[24] Jeremiah 26:3
[25] 2 Thessalonians 2: 1-3
[26] Revelation 12:11

Chapter One

[27] Acts 2:16
[28] Matthew 24:33-34
[29] Ecclesiastes 8:5
[30] Luke 21:26
[31] Matthew 24:34
[32] 2 Peter 3: 3-14
[33] Mark 13:23
[34] Luke 21: 11, 25-26
[35] Luke 21:26
[36] Mark 13:32
[37] Matthew 24: 32-35
[38] Matthew 24:3
[39] Mark 13:23
[40] Matthew 24: 4-15, 33-35
[41] Matthew 24:33

Chapter Two

[42] Genesis 6:3
[43] Genesis 15:13
[44] Numbers 14:33
[45] Jeremiah 29:10
[46] Daniel 11:32, 12:10
[47] Daniel 9:25-26a
[48] Jeremiah 30:3
[49] Isaiah 43:6
[50] Leviticus 26:32
[51] Jeremiah 25: 12
[52] Jeremiah 51:1
[53] Jeremiah 50:9
[54] Jeremiah 50:9
[55] Jeremiah 4:13
[56] Joel 3: 1-2
[57] Daniel 11:19
[58] Daniel 12:4
[59] Daniel 12:4
[60] Matthew 24:37
[61] Genesis 6:5
[62] 2 Timothy 3: 1-7

Chapter Three

[63] Matthew 24:15
[64] Matthew 24:15
[65] Matthew 24:15
[66] Genesis 6: 1-2
[67] Genesis 6:4
[68] Daniel 10: 13-14
[69] Matthew 24:15
[70] 2 Peter 3:10
[71] 2 Peter 1: 19-21
[72] Daniel 11:33
[73] Daniel 7: 13-14
[74] Matthew 24:22

Chapter Four

[75] Colossians 2:17
[76] 1 Thessalonians 5:4

Chapter Five

[77] Isaiah 48:3
[78] Genesis 1:31
[79] Genesis 2: 1-3
[80] Jude 1: 14-15
[81] Ecclesiastes 3:1
[82] Isaiah 44:6-7
[83] Genesis 1: 1-3, 31
[84] 2 Peter 3:8, italics added
[85] Matthew 10:26
[86] Job 11:6
[87] Ecclesiastes 3: 14-15
[88] Daniel 8:19
[89] 2 Peter 3: 11-13
[90] Luke 21:25
[91] Matthew 24:21
[92] Revelation 21:1,5

Chapter Six

[93] Genesis 6:3
[94] Genesis 7:11-12
[95] Matthew 24:37
[96] Matthew 24:37
[97] Luke 4:19
[98] 2 Peter 3:3-7
[99] Matthew 24:37
[100] Psalm 90:12
[101] Mark 13:23
[102] Jeremiah 23:19-20
[103] Psalm 25:14
[104] Job 11:6
[105] Matthew 24:37
[106] Matthew 24:15
[107] Matthew 24:22
[108] Luke 21:28
[109] Matthew 24:29-31
[110] Matthew 22:1-14
[111] John 14: 1-3
[112] John 3: 3-8, 36
[113] Revelation 20:15

Chapter Seven

[114] Daniel 10:14
[115] Daniel 12:4
[116] Daniel 12: 9-10
[117] Daniel 11:33-35
[118] Daniel 9: 21-23
[119] Daniel 10: 11-14
[120] Daniel 12:6

Chapter Eight

[121] Daniel 2:31-35
[122] Daniel 2:34
[123] Daniel 2:41-45
[124] Daniel 2:34
[125] Daniel 2:41-45
[126] Revelation 13:16-18
[127] Ezekiel 38 & 39
[128] Ezekiel 38:1-2, 10-12
[129] Daniel 8:23-24
[130] Daniel 8:24-25

Chapter Nine

[131] Matthew 24:15
[132] Daniel 12:10
[133] 1 Thessalonians 5:5
[134] Daniel 11:33
[135] 1 Thessalonians 5:4

Chapter Ten

[136] Daniel 9:25-26
[137] Daniel 12: 11-12
[138] Matthew 24:15
[139] Matthew 24:15
[140] Daniel 12: 11-12

Chapter Eleven

[141] Daniel 12:11-12
[142] Daniel 12:12
[143] Matthew 24:22
[144] Daniel 12:1
[145] Daniel 12:10

Chapter Twelve

[146] Daniel 9: 25-26
[147] Daniel 9:24
[148] Daniel 12:12
[149] Matthew 24:7
[150] Zechariah 12:1-3
[151] Romans 11:26
[152] Zechariah 9:16
[153] Daniel 12:2
[154] Revelation 20:5-6
[155] Revelation 20:12
[156] Revelation 20:15
[157] Ezekiel 42:20
[158] Revelation 11:1-2
[159] Daniel 9:24
[160] Daniel 12:1

Chapter Thirteen

[161] Daniel 8:9
[162] Jeremiah 30:7
[163] Revelation 13:4-8
[164] Daniel 9:27
[165] 2 Thessalonians 2:3-4,8

Chapter Fourteen

[166] Daniel 9:25-26
[167] Luke 19:42-44
[168] Daniel 8: 9-12
[169] Revelation 13:14-15
[170] Revelation 11: 1-2
[171] 2 Thessalonians 2:4-8
[172] Zechariah 14:3-4
[173] Daniel 8:14
[174] Zechariah 12:9-12
[175] Daniel 8:14
[176] Daniel 9:24
[177] Revelation 12:6
[178] Daniel 12:7
[179] Revelation 13:5,7
[179] John 9:4

Chapter Fifteen

[181] Daniel 11:40
[182] Matthew 24:7-8
[183] Psalm 91
[184] 1 Peter 1:13
[185] Revelation 13:16-18

Chapter Sixteen

[186] Revelation 16:8-9
[187] Joel 2:30-31
[188] Luke 21:25
[189] Revelation 6:12-13
[190] Revelation 8:12
[191] Ecclesiastes 3:1
[192] Joel 2:10
[193] Luke 21:11
[194] Revelation 12: 1,5
[195] Genesis 1:14
[196] Psalm 19:1
[197] Joel 2:10
[198] Acts 2:20
[199] Luke 21:25
[200] Matthew 24:6-8

Chapter Seventeen

[201] Ezekiel 42:20
[202] Revelation 11: 1-2
[203] Ezekiel 43:2
[204] Ezekiel 43: 4-7
[205] 2 Thessalonians 2: 4,8
[206] Revelation 13: 14-15
[207] Luke 21: 20-27
[208] Isaiah 63: 1-4
[209] Revelation 19: 11-21

Chapter Eighteen

[210] Genesis 1:26
[211] 1 John 3:2
[212] Revelation 5:9-10
[213] Daniel 7:27
[214] Deuteronomy 30:3
[215] Deuteronomy 32:15
[216] Daniel 11:37-38
[217] Isaiah 28:14-15

[218] Daniel 9:27
[219] Jeremiah 25:12
[220] Revelation 18:2
[221] Luke 17:28

Chapter Nineteen

[222] Genesis 31: 38
[223] Judges 4:3
[224] 1 Samuel 7:2
[225] Matthew 3:16-17
[226] Hosea 6: 1-3

Chapter Twenty

[227] Revelation 3:10
[228] 1 Thessalonians 5:9
[229] Daniel 11:35
[230] Hebrews 12: 6-8, 11
[231] Philippians 1:6
[232] Luke 17:34-37
[233] Matthew 24:28
[234] Revelation 19:14-21
[235] Luke 17:37
[236] Ezekiel 39: 17-20
[237] Luke 17: 34-36
[238] Joel 3:2
[239] Matthew 13:24-30, 38-41
[240] Matthew 13:30
[241] Psalm 104:35
[242] Revelation 3:10
[243] Revelation 20:4-6
[244] Revelation 22:18
[245] 1 Corinthians 15:51
[246] Psalm 91:1, 5-11
[247] Isaiah 26:20
[248] Daniel 12:1
[249] Daniel 11:32
[250] Philippians 4:13
[251] John 17: 14-19
[252] Isaiah 59:19b
[253] Matthew 24: 29-31
[254] 1 Thessalonians 5:3
[255] Revelation 3:10
[256] Matthew 24:29
[257] 1 John 4:4
[258] Isaiah 43:2

Chapter Twenty - continued

259   Isaiah 54:17
260   Romans 8:18
261   Daniel 11:32-35
262   Malachi 4: 1-3
263   Ezekiel 39: 17-21
264   Revelation 19:17-19
265   Ezekiel 39:9
266   John 9:4a
267   Daniel 11:32
268   John 14:12
269   Revelation 3:10
270   Daniel 11:32
271   1 Corinthians 2:9
272   1 Corinthians 2:10
273   Daniel 11:32
274   Romans 8: 19-22
275   Joel 2: 28-29
276   Philippians 3:13
277   Ephesians 4:13
278   Revelation 12: 7-11
279   Romans 8:1
280   Hebrews 10:38
281   Romans 8:19
282   Ephesians 1:23
283   Acts 2: 34-35
284   Acts 3: 20-21
285   Romans 8:37
286   Matthew 16:18
287   Hebrews 1:14
288   Psalm 91: 11-12
289   1 Peter 1:4
290   Colossians 1:13
291   Acts 3:21
292   Ephesians 3: 18-19
293   Mark 16:20
294   Revelation 12:11
295   Acts 2: 34-35
296   John 19:30
297   Romans 8:37
298   John 15:1-5
299   Ephesians 1:23
300   Ephesians 4:13
301   1 Corinthians 2:9
302   John 14:12
303   Daniel 11:32
304   1 Corinthians 15: 45-49
305   1 Corinthians 15:49

[306] Ephesians 3:19
[307] Acts 3:21
[308] Mark 9:23
[309] Joel 1:4
[310] John 17:22
[311] Matthew 24:14
[312] 1 Corinthians 2:9
[313] Hebrews 12:26
[314] Ephesians 4:13
[315] Matthew 16:18
[316] Luke 10:19
[317] Joel 3:14
[318] Isaiah 59:19
[319] Joel 2:23
[320] Amos 9:13
[321] 1 John 4:4
[322] Romans 8:37
[323] 2 Thessalonians 3:3
[324] Amos 9:13
[325] Mathew 24:14

Chapter Twenty One

[326] Acts 1: 9-10
[327] 1 Thessalonians 4: 16-17
[328] Matthew 16:28
[329] Philippians 3:12-14
[330] 1 Thessalonians 5:9
[331] Matthew 24: 32-35
[332] Matthew 24:33
[333] 2 Corinthians 5:1, 6-8
[334] 2 Corinthians 5:8
[335] Revelation 14:13
[336] Revelation 19:11-21
[337] Zechariah 14:4
[338] Isaiah 59:20
[339] Zechariah 12:10

Chapter Twenty Two

[340] Revelation 20:1-3
[341] Revelation 20:6
[342] Revelation 21:5
[343] Revelation 20: 7-10
[344] 2 Peter 3:7
[345] 2 Peter 3: 10-12
[346] Revelation 20: 11-15
[347] Revelation 21: 1-6

Chapter Twenty Two - continued

[348] Revelation 21: 1-2
[349] Revelation 21: 10-14
[350] Revelation 21: 22-27
[351] Revelation 21:5-7

Conclusion

[352] Luke 19:13b
[353] Luke 21:18
[354] Psalm 91:1-11

The Way of Salvation

[355] Romans 3:23
[356] Romans 6:23
[357] Romans 5:8
[358] Romans 10:13
[359] Romans 10:9
[360] 1 John 5:1a
[361] 1 John 5:13

BIBLIOGRAPHY

Artapanus, Hellenistic - Jewish History, B.C. 100
The Epistle of Barnabas 100 B.C.
Halafta Rabbi Yose ben, Seder Olam Rabbah, A.D. 150
The Mishna
Africanus Julius, The Chronographies, A.D. 170
Clement of Alexandria, The Stromata, A.D. 194
Irenaeus, Against Heresies, A.D. 180
Tertullian, Answers to Jews, A.D. 198
MoLad Tohu, Rabbinical Chronology
The Chronographer of the Year 354
The Book of Jubilees
The Book of Enoch
Eusebius, The Chronicles of Eusebius
Josephus
Mommson Chronica Minora
Dionysius the Little, Dionysius Exiguus ,A.D. 525
Bishop Ussher, The Annals of History
John W. Parker, A Treatise on Chronology of the Scriptures, A.D. 1844
Robert T. Beckwith, A Key to Chronology of the New Testament A.D. 1865
Hodden and Strounghton, Bearing on the Recent Discovery of the
Trustworthiness of the New Testament, A.D. 1915
Foundation of Biblical Research, The Birth of Jesus Recalculated A.D. 1978
Jack Finegan, Handbook of Biblical Chronology, A.F. 1964
Spencer Iowa, History, Harmony, The Exile and Return, A.D. 1986
Spencer Iowa, Bible Chrononology and Scientific Method, A.D. 1988
Rabbi Menachem Kohen, Prophecies for the Era of Muslim Terror, A.D. 2007
Encyclopedia Britannica
Encyclopedia Judaica

A MONTHLY PROPHETIC UPDATE

CHRONOGRAM REPORT

WWW.WRNORADIO.COM

Email: wrnoradio@mailup.net

NOTES

NOTES